Praise for

CREATIVE TIME MANAGEMENT FOR THE NEW MILLENNIUM

by Jan Yager

"In an age when everyone seems to have too much to do and too little time to do it, this thorough, well-written guide will enable you to get more done, and feel better doing it. The last chapter alone ("125 Top Time-Saving Ideas") is worth the price of the whole book."

—Mark Sanborn, CSP, CPAE, author and seminar leader

"To get control of your time, your work, your technical gadgets, and your personal life, read *Creative Time Management for the New Millennium*. The practical hands-on advice will repay you many times over."

—Michael LeBoeuf, Ph.D., author, *Working Smart*

"Here's an excellent super-guide to gaining control over your time and your life."

—Lucy H. Hedrick, author, *Five Days to an Organized Life*

"A pragmatic, easy to digest road map to true understanding of effectively managing your precious resource of time."

—Bob Danzig, former President, Hearst Newspapers

"The ideas and insights in *Creative Time Management for the New Millennium* will transform your hectic life into an organized journey."

—Glenna Salsbury, CSP, CPAE, author and professional speaker

Selected Nonfiction Books by Jan Yager, Ph.D.
(a/k/a J. L. Barkas/Janet Lee Barkas)

Making Your Office Work for You

Business Protocol

How to Write Like a Professional

Friendshifts®: The Power of Friendship and How It Shapes Our Lives

Single in America

The Help Book

Victims

The Vegetable Passion: A History of the Vegetarian State of Mind

CREATIVE TIME MANAGEMENT FOR THE NEW MILLENNIUM

Become More Productive and Still Have Time For Fun

**Second edition
Completely revised and updated**

Jan Yager, Ph.D.

Hannacroix Creek Books, Inc.   Stamford, CT

Published by Hannacroix Creek Books, Inc.
1127 High Ridge Road
PMB 110
Stamford, CT 06905-1203
ISBN: 0-7394-0631-0
Printed in the USA.

Dedicated to my husband, Fred;
our sons, Scott and Jeffrey;
my mother; my sister, Eileen;
my extended family; my friends;
my colleagues, clients, and readers;
and the memory of
my father and my brother

Author's Note and Disclaimer

I have retained from the first edition of this book whatever classic guidelines are still valid today. I substituted more contemporary examples and added new information and concepts based on the original research I have conducted, and the seminars and lectures I have delivered. For example, to bring the basic time management information of the 1st edition into the new millennium, I distributed an extensive work survey completed by 234 working men and women throughout the United States and in more than a dozen countries. (For more details about my credentials, see About the Author on the last page of this book.)

Quotes in this book not attributed to a secondary source are from the original research conducted by the author, in the form of either interviews or questionnaires, and are reprinted verbatim and, if necessary, excerpted. If editing of a quote was required for either sense or clarification, those additions or changes are indicated by brackets.

If anonymity was requested, a fictitious first name has been provided; identifying details have also been changed to maintain that anonymity. However, care has been taken to preserve the integrity of each example.

Secondary sources cited within the text have complete bibliographic entries in the Bibliography.

The purpose of this book is to provide inspiration, information, and opinions on the topics covered. It is sold with the understanding that neither the publisher nor the author are engaged in rendering psychological, medical, sociological, legal, or other professional services.

Typographical or content mistakes may be unwittingly contained in this book. In addition, information may be out of date because it was unavailable until after the date of the book's completion, printing, or distribution.

The author and publisher shall have neither liability nor responsibility to any person or entity with regard to any loss or damage caused, or alleged to be caused, directly or indirectly by the opinions or information contained in this book.

Contents

CONTENTS

CONTENTS

1
Creative Time Management: An Introduction

Lost time is never found again.
—BENJAMIN FRANKLIN (*Poor Richard's Almanac*)

What is Creative Time Management?

Managing your time well means managing your life well. People who handle their time well do it creatively. They show certain characteristics that separate them from those who are usually in a state of unprepared frenzy. They make short- and long-term plans, set and keep realistic schedules, take efficient and timely breaks, and view tasks to be done as opportunities rather than dreaded obligations. They practice creative time management by taking control of their time and therefore their life.

We are not all endowed with brilliance, good looks, or lots of money, but we each get the same number of hours every day. A great deal may be achieved in those 24 hours, or not much at all. It is up to you to make optimum use of those hours.

What Are the Benefits of Creative Time Management?

The most important benefit of creative time management is

that it enables you to feel in control of your life. Those who feel in control of their lives experience less stress, are more relaxed, productive, self-satisfied, and live longer.

Poor time management causes missed deadlines, unfinished projects, disappointed employers, annoyed clients, cancelled appointments, and unfulfilled career aspirations. It can also lead to heightened tension, anger, embarrassment, low self-esteem, and depression. It can cause problems in marriage or romantic relationships as busy couples find there is never enough time to be intimate or spend quality time together. It can be a factor in children growing up strangers to their parents, or potential friendships that never progress beyond acquaintanceships.

In the years I have been researching time management, I discovered a common time management problem shared by those who are usually busy but rarely able to accomplish as much as they want to or know they are capable of achieving: They are *reactive*, rather than *active*, persons. They react to external demands on them, whether for a report due on Friday or a party they are invited to on Saturday, rather than acting according to long-term goals they have set for themselves within which most short-term decisions are made.

Furthermore, the necessity to prioritize what is important usually becomes clear when they get attacks of "if only" ("I wouldn't have been late if only I hadn't answered the phone on my way out," "If only I hadn't started working on that other assignment before I finished rewriting that report") as well as during those moments of pride when the rewards are most obvious — having work done on time, getting to a meeting on time, getting promoted, finishing an in-depth training program, being asked to make a presentation about what you do, publishing a book, feeling in control and on top of your work or family demands.

Through my interviews, observations, and research, I have discovered that most men and women share the same goal: a full life, not a life that is weighted too heavily toward work, family, or leisure activities. The man who never exercises or does anything for himself (until he has a heart attack) because he is attending only to his job and family is someone in need of creative time management as much as the woman who is juggling all her commitments so vigorously—spouse, job, children—that she lacks a moment to put up her feet and just relax.

Could Your Time Management Skills Use Improvement?

To help you determine just how productive you really are, take this five-question self-evaluation. On a piece of paper, or on your computer, answer each question with a *yes, no,* or *sometimes.*

1. Do you make a conscientious effort to separate urgent matters from other demands?
2. Do you take the time to do enough background research so you can make the best possible decisions?
3. Do you allocate at least one hour each day for uninterrupted time for thinking, reading, planning, or creative work?
4. Do you spend sufficient time developing and maintaining business and personal relationships?
5. Do you work hard to do your best—rather than measuring yourself by a standard equated with unattainable perfection?

If you answered *yes* to all five questions, at least on these five issues your time management skills are excellent.

If you answered *no* or *sometimes* to one or more questions, you will benefit by improving your time management skills.

You may already suspect that how you handle your time could be enhanced since you are probably more stressed than you would like to be, busier than usual though getting less done, or finding yourself saying, more and more often, "I just don't have the time."

Read on. You will find knowledge, skills, and help in the pages that follow to give you the competitive edge, and peace of mind, that creative time management provides.

Fortunately You **Can** *Change How You Manage Your Time*

Slogans—"Make every day count," "Live each day as if it were your last," "Life is a process, not an event"—provide overall philosophies. However, those phrases do not tell you *how* to apply those philosophies to daily life.

Creative Time Management for the New Millennium will help you pinpoint how you currently manage your time, how you would like to manage it, what's stopping you, and ways to achieve your "ideal" for work, school, or leisure hours.

There will certainly be times in your life when you feel breathless, frenzied, and driven by how little time you feel you have to do all that you want to do, or to be with the people you want to be with. But if you pause long enough to apply to your day the time management techniques that work – prioritizing, breaking huge tasks into manageable pieces, dealing effectively with telephone calls or E-mail, understanding what is behind a specific time management obstacle that slows you down, such as an inability to say "no", so you can overcome it – you will more quickly gain control of yourself, your demands, and your time.

Less stress is definitely an outcome of better time management; effectively managing your time will certainly help you accomplish more, in less time, at work as well as help you make better decisions about what to do with your time in the first place.

Initially there may be frustrations when you take charge of your life and time, but this is only temporary. Fortunately you will quickly see benefits as well, not to mention the permanent and greater long-term gains. This is not the same thing as becoming so narcissistic that everything and everyone is measured by "What does this time demand mean to me?" Sometimes, for example, it may be in your best interest to put others before yourself, sometimes not. Example: You are working on an important assignment. The phone rings. Your friend is upset and wants to talk for ten minutes. You say you don't have the time. Your friend is disappointed. You have that ten minutes for your work, but in the long run, was working on your report the best use of those ten minutes? A creative way to handle that same situation might be to say to your friend, "I have a deadline so I can't talk now. When could I call you back tonight so we could talk?"

The goal of this book is to help you make those crucial judgments about how you spend your time. As each day is spent more efficiently and creatively, you will achieve more in the short run, as well as attaining more of your long-range work and personal goals. That will all add up to a more fulfilling life.

How one manages one's time will depend on where one is in one's life cycle, which, today, has a wider variation than even, say, twenty years ago. A thirty-two-year old woman gives up her job in Manhattan as a magazine editor to begin medical school in Colorado. A sixty-year-old man gives up smoking and devotes more time to exercise than at any time since high school. A thirty-eight-year-old man, a new father, considers trading his freelance writing career for the steady pay check of a corporate position. A forty-year-old woman, faced with her teenager's imminent departure from home, thinks about what full-time work she now wants to do. A twenty-two-year-old college senior wonders if she should get a public relations job or attend graduate school.

There are practical tips in this book about managing your time that will help you spend your time more productively. Used wisely, the phone can be a terrific time saver; for many of us, it wastes hours of time, interrupting projects and in-person conversations. Doing the paper shuffle can consume valuable time; managing your files well could be a time saver. Getting organized refers to such specific techniques as creating an effective "things to do" list; it also involves learning more basic organizing principles that will help you to organize your life, not just your books and files.

Workaholism

Workaholism is often a symptom of poor time management: an inability to begin, pursue, and complete a project leads the workaholic to focus solely on the project. The squeaky wheel gets all the grease and the other wheels get none; the job becomes all. As one reluctant workaholic somewhat breathlessly put it, "I keep working around the clock because I hope somehow I'll get everything done so someday I won't have to work so hard." Pacing yourself, and gaining control of your time, lets you accomplish what you value at work, in school, or at home, and gives you more time for friends, family, and leisure activities. It also helps avert burnout—total loss of initiative or of the ability to continue work toward accomplishing the task at hand. Poor time management can cause the burnout syndrome; even if some key goals are achieved, it is only at enormous personal and professional cost.

Judy, 44, a working mother of two teenagers, was interviewed while on vacation for a week with several women coworkers and friends: "I work in the hospital's maternity ward as a nurse-midwife six days a week, and at the supermarket Saturdays, and on my day off. My children are in high school now, so they can take care of themselves, and my husband's fairly self-sufficient. I like the work I do and I'm never bored. I'm glad I went back to school at age forty, even though, at the time, everyone thought I was crazy."

Judy initially sounded like an effective and rewarded manager of her time. And while she's at work, she is. But upon further questioning, it appeared that not having a set routine while on vacation disoriented her. She finds waking up at seven every day, and having a set number of tasks to perform, more "relaxing" than the unstructured environment of a week in the sun. Judy may be an achiever, but it appears to have cost her a great deal. She is severely overweight, smokes, and a compulsive talker.

We all know people like Judy, competent in one setting, but tense and insecure in others, and we strive for life management that is effective in a variety of work and leisure settings.

Pacing Yourself

Warren, 32, a health care professional, is able to take off Wednesdays during the week. He also never works weekends, unless there is an emergency. "Taking Wednesdays off gives me the ability, energy, and incentive to do my best when I am at work," he explains. "It makes a difference." Sometimes his friends suggest that he would earn more money by working more days; he feels it might be a short-lived gain, since the quality of his work might suffer, along with his job satisfaction.

A freelance researcher has similarly evolved a professionally and personally satisfying work routine. Because his job is physically and emotionally demanding, requiring intense concentration and long hours in front of his computer, he works in two- to three-hour stretches. He uses rest periods to go running, play tennis, place or return phone calls, do grocery shopping, and similar tasks unrelated to work. In this way, he is able to put in twelve-to-fourteen hour work days in his home-based office with enthusiasm and without physical or mental exhaustion. His pattern is the opposite of those heading toward burnout who work like crazy for days, months, even years, tuning out most other considerations only to find, once the project is finished, or their energy is completely diminished, they need weeks, months, or sometimes years to sort out the resultant mess in their lives (and to their health).

Those who work in outside offices are also trying to pace themselves better. Job sharing or flexible hours is becoming more acceptable with time working at home or time on the road counting as a day's work. Those who work away from an outside office, if they are able to handle the social or business isolation it may cause, often remark how much more productive they are without the constant interruptions that they had to cope with in the office.

Being effective, whether you work in an outside office, travel a great deal for your job, or work in a home office, does not always mean working longer hours, or even harder. It may even mean working fewer hours; it may mean changing where and when you work, or it may mean trying to do something in a different way.

Consider a married woman, 29, who had her first child last year. A child care worker looks after the infant while she and her husband are at their offices. Before the baby was born, she was in her office by eight, and did not leave till 6:30 or 7:00 each evening. Now, because of the baby, she does not arrive till nine, and always leaves by 5:00. "I'm amazed that I don't find that my productivity has suffered," she told me. "A lot of that early and late stuff was for show. The only difference now is that I return more phone calls the next day, rather than right away, but I've found the calls can wait until the next day." Although some managers may disagree about the wisdom of letting calls wait, she feels she has adjusted her time to manage her work- and home-related responsibilities more effectively, even though she now has more demands on her time.

For her, the key to her creative time management was her ability to set – and work toward – clear goals in both her professional and personal life. The other key for her was learning her limitations: the thesis she had been writing to complete her master's degree had to be put aside for a year. "I'll get back to it," she says confidently and convincingly.

Technology and Time Management

Over the last decade, there have been numerous changes in the every day world of work, most notably technological advances, such as the widespread use of personal computers and fax machines, the popular use of the Internet, E-mail, cell (mobile) phones, and beepers. With the Internet, we all now have the ability to communicate instantaneously with others, near or far. But for some, the Internet has actually become their new time problem, as they spend hours each day "on line," neglecting their business priorities or even their family obligations.

Because of technology, more is now expected of us in terms of the quality of our work, how much we can accomplish, as well as the speed with which we can achieve or produce it. But technology can only improve our efficiency so far. Word processors or computers may facilitate the physical act of writing or typing and editing or rewriting, but the creative part, the inspiration, the unique way of expressing thoughts and ideas, is still up to each individual, and it unfolds in as mysterious a way as it did before.

Look at the multitude of ways that technology has made it possible to communicate with each other beyond the traditional telephone. Cell (mobile) phones have brought telephone service to people in remote areas who were cut off from telephone service in the past. Beepers enable sending a message to someone who is on the road or away from a telephone. However, beepers and cell phones have made it easier to be interrupted, 24 hours a day, including weekends and holidays, necessitating even greater control over how you self-manage your time than ever before.

Advertising executive Charles Peebler reminds us all about the human element that is still pivotal despite technology:

> Clearly, technology, from computers to executive "toys," has changed the landscape of communications. And I use most of the available tools. But I remain *insistent* that on key issues--matters of urgency and sensitivity, when nuance and judgment are criticial-- that nothing beats *face-to-face* discussion.

The Internet is a valuable tool to quickly access research and information to augment or replace time-consuming research trips. However, regular library visits are still irreplaceable social, community, and intellectual meeting centers for youth and adults.

There is also an information explosion because of technology—there are just more books being written, more information available that needs to be read and digested.

Word processors and computers have made it mandatory to have "letter-perfect" correspondence but perfection is time consuming, and often with little or no support staff to make those changes. Why not just pick up the phone and call to avoid such formalities? Because writing a formal letter on good quality letterhead may be preferred, not calling or sending a fax or E-mail.

Creative Time Management for the New Millennium will help you to spend each day more efficiently as you achieve more in the short-run and more of your long-range goals. That combination will add up to a more successful career and a more fulfilling and less-stressful life. Since most everyone agrees that "time is money," improving your time management skills is a wise use of your time.

The next chapter is a presentation and discussion of the 7 principles of creative time management.

2
The 7 Principles of Creative Time Management

Here are the fundamental principles of creative time management:

1. Be Active, Not Reactive.

Make *active* decisions about how you spend your time instead of *reacting* to every demand on you, whether it is someone calling you on the phone at that very moment or being asked to become membership chair for your professional association.

You decide what is important to you, and you say "no" to anything that intereferes.

It will be much easier to be active if you also follow principle #2, namely, setting goals.

2. Set Goals.

By setting goals you know where you are going. Goals are necessary, at work, school, or play. Without them you flounder, and react erratically to opportunities and problems, with little perspective on the effects they will have on your personal and professional life.

Do you have a grand scheme? At certain times in life it's easier to realize that you need a master plan—for example, when you're in high school or college and practically everyone is making major life decisions—where to go to school, or what subjects or career to pursue. Once a path is decided upon, law school or acting, for example, and once a career is started, it's easy to get caught up in earning a living, dating or marrying, and raising a family. The time for a "grand scheme" may seem to be behind you.

It's not! No matter what age you are, you can develop daily, weekly, yearly, or longer-range goals to guide you. That does not mean becoming such a future-oriented person that you fail to enjoy the present. What it does mean is that by setting goals you can better manage your time and life today.

3. Prioritize actions.

Once you establish your goals, you need to prioritize your activities to achieve those goals. Prioritizing means creating a plan of action. Keep in mind the principle of nineteenth-century Italian economist and sociologist Vilfredo Pareto, Pareto's 80/20 principle, that 20 percent of what you do will give you 80 percent of your results. The key to prioritizing is carefully identifying the right 20 percent of your activities, and making them priorities.

Prioritizing, creating specific goals for each day or hour, and then accomplishing each task before going on to the next, will also help overcome the "I'm doing too much as once" syndrome.

Keep in mind that prioritizing may be stressful since it means putting some people or things ahead of others to get the priority job done.

4. Keep your focus.

Maximize your productivity by concentrating on one major project at a time. Once you have set your goals and prioritized your actions, stay on track until that project is completed. Whatever it is you're doing, give it your all.

Try to simplify your goals, and set short-range priorities, by dividing your goal into a noun and a verb. Just two words. If it's more than two or three words, you may be the victim of muddy thinking or goal overload — wanting to accomplish too many goals at once, and juggling too many demands on you simultaneously, you are encouraging yourself to fail at any one of them.

Sometimes the verb-noun principle is cloudy; if you are dissatisfied at the office, you have to clarify your verb-noun principle to improve your situation. Is it "get a raise?" "Change departments?" "Work shorter hours?" "Vary duties?"

Once you decide on your verb-noun principle, you can consider the actions you need to do that will aid your achievement of that goal. Whatever you do (how you spend your time) should be in the service of fulfilling your verb-noun goal.

5. Create realistic deadlines.

Deadlines, especially if realistic, help keep you focused on specific long-term goals and especially on short-term priorities. You should not dread a deadline but welcome it. If someone else does not impose a deadline on you and your work, create deadlines for yourself.

It is also useful to create a to-do list of projects or goals, but you also have to estimate how long it will take you to complete each task so you can specify concrete deadlines. If you have done a similar task in the past, consider how long it took you previously. If this project is new, your estimates may be more ideal than real. (If you are like most people, you probably underestimate completion time, especially if it involves research, writing, creativity, or working with others. Add ten to twenty percent to your estimate so you are more likely to come out on time.)

6. D-O I-T N-O-W.

Once you decide on a plan and are focused, just do it *now*.

Here is an easy way to help you remember this principle:

D = Divide and conquer what you have to do.

Break big tasks into little tasks and give each part of that task a realistic deadline.

O = Organize your materials, how you will do it.

I = Ignore interruptions that are annoying distractions.

T = Take the time to learn how to do things yourself.

N = Now, not tomorrow. Don't procrastinate.

O = Opportunity is knocking. Take advantage of opportunities.

W = Watch out for time gobblers. Keep track of, and in control of, how much time you spend on the Internet, reading and sending E-mails, watching TV, or talking on the phone.

7. *Balance your life.*

The 7th principle means creating time for yourself as well as for those you care about--romantic partner, children, parents, siblings, extended family, friends, neighbors, volunteer groups, colleagues, even pets. While becoming more productive at work is certainly a worthwhile goal, having a fuller, more productive and balanced life is even better. So remember to apply these creative time management principles not only to work, but to relationships and leisure activities as well.

The next chapter will examine ten key obstacles to creative time management and how to overcome them.

3
Overcoming
10 Key Obstacles to
Managing Your Time

Procrastination is the thief of time.
    EDWARD YOUNG (*Night Thoughts*)

A common misconception about time is that you can waste it. You can't waste time, but you can mismanage it. This chapter examines 10 ways people mismanage their time, providing possible solutions for overcoming those tendencies.

Doing Too Much At Once

I recently conducted a survey of 234 working men and women to determine how people mismanage their time. I was sure the number one way was going to be procrastination. But that came in a distant second (8%), and virtually tied with the 3rd, 4th, and 5th reasons, namely an inability to say "no," paperwork, and perfectionism.

The #1 reason given for mismanaging time by the most people was "trying to do too much at once" (33%).

If you think you have too many things to do, you're probably right.

Of course we all have many things to do. The key is how to get everything you have to do accomplished effectively and efficiently in as systematic a way as possible.

Where most run into trouble is when you try to do everything at once so nothing gets done; then you feel like a miserable failure.

You know your situations, your capacities, and your limitations best. As one working woman put it, "I take on so much that all of a sudden I just feel panicked, and I start screwing everything up."

Take on as many tasks as you can competently handle and still meet your deadlines. For some, it's only one; for others, two or three. You need to critically assess your limits and capabilities.

If you have the tendency to do too many things at once, you will have to recognize it, understand it, and force yourself to finish obligations before you begin new ones.

Here are tips to deal with "doing too much at once":

Solution #1 - Prioritize all you have to do in a list, with the most important thing first.

Solution #2 -   Use your list to focus on doing one thing at a time.

Solution #3 - Do not start the next task until you've completed the first one.

Solution #4 -   Use selective attention.

If you need variety in what you do, rather than sticking to only one job until it is completed, consider the time effective way that the late Isaac Asimov, author of more than 280 books, coped with that by practicing selective attention. He had four major projects that he worked on "at once," but when he was working on any one of those four projects, that one project—whatever stage it was in— had his full attention. (For some, however, shifting gears and going back and forth among several projects throws them off. In that

*roject-till-finished rule may be what's needed.)
...y, to overcome your "doing too much at once"
...ioritize, creating clear, specific goals for each day,
...our (or period) of the day, accomplishing each goal or
...re going on to the next one. Decide which tasks require
your ..clusive attention and which ones you can do simultaneously.
You can listen to the radio while driving your car, but you can't
read the newspaper. You can read the newspaper or watch TV while
working out on a stationary bicycle, but you probably couldn't
read a complicated technical report while exercising.

The Inability to Say "No"

Quite often, behind the "doing too many things at once" syndrome
is someone who can't say "no." Saying "yes" when you should say
"no" arises from the childish wish to please everyone, and represents
a failure to adequately define what's important to you. It's hard to
say "no." You may fear an opportunity will never come again, or
that saying "no" will hurt someone's feelings forever.

Solution #1 - Simplify your goals.

Saying " no"—gracefully—is a two-step process. You decide what
your needs and limits are, and then you say "no" to whatever
interferes.

You are saying " no" because whatever is asked of you is not
the best use of your time right now.

Solution #2 - Practice saying "no" in a way that is kind, gentle, and positive.

It's not the fact that you're saying "no" that usually alienates
someone, but *how* you express yourself. Tell the truth but be
diplomatic not cruel, express your gratitude for the invitation and,
if appropriate, suggest another time to get together, or when to get
back to you when you might say "yes" or at least reconsider your

"no."

Solution #3 - Desensitize yourself to the word "no."

What do you do if you just can't say the word "no"? The word just never seems to come out of your mouth (although after you get off the phone, or later on, you wish it had).

Write the word in big letters by your telephone or computer, or on the desk where you answer your mail. Don't be wishy washy and say "maybe" if a tactful and firm "no" is what's needed.

Solution #4 - Be clear you are saying "no" to a request but not rejecting the person making the request.

When you do mean "No, never," you can reject the request without dismissing the person asking it. Too often someone with a problem of saying "no" gracefully turns against the person who makes the demand. (A variation on the "blame the messenger for the bad news" syndrome.)

Solution #5 - Handle it as a "No, not this, but..."

If at all possible, turning a flat "no" into a "No, not this, but" may be a good time saver because it enables you to turn almost any "no" situation into an opportunity. Example: after a job interview, you decide this is not the right position for you. How you handle "No, not this, but" may mean the difference between the interaction between you and the interviewer leading to a dead-end versus turning it into a possible future opportunity. You may want to impress the interviewer so that she might someday consider you for a job that is for you. Or you may want to ensure a positive report about you to the referral or employment agency, which will then try even harder to work on your behalf.

The situations to which "No, not this, but" applies are innumerable. You are being considered for a teaching position but making a commitment to a weekly class is not possible right now because of your other responsibilities. You handle the "no" in such a positive way that a year later, after another networking "hello, this is what I'm up to" phone call, you are invited, for a fee, to teach several classes for just one day.

Creatively handling "No, not this, but" encounters will enable you to turn chances that are less than ideal into options – now or in the future. Most important of all, it will help you overcome your inability to say "no" (which probably gets you into a "doing too much at once" syndrome.)

Procrastination

Procrastination means putting off until tomorrow anything that you are supposed to do today. But the very act of delay may have consequences; if you delay making airline reservations long enough you may be forced to take a 6 a.m. flight because everything else is booked or, worse yet, have to take a train or drive (if that is even feasible) because everything is booked. If you miss the deadline for a conference, the registration fee may be much higher, or registration may be filled and closed out so you are unable to attend at all. If you wait so long before you start a project that you lack adequate time to do a good job on it, you've given yourself a less than optimal chance to succeed.

Here are several solutions for overcoming procrastination:

Solution #1 - Make whatever you are procrastinating about the very first task you do that day.

Force yourself to do what you have to do first thing in the morning, as soon as you wake up, or as your first task at work, before going on to anything else. "Hold all calls" if necessary till you get that project or commitment done.

Solution #2 - Try the reward system.

Make sure the reward that you decide on is something you truly enjoy so you'll have the motivation to keep at your necessary task.

Solution #3 - Try creative procrastination.

Another solution to procrastination is *creative procrastination*. It's creative because it helps you to achieve your overall goal by reordering short-term priorities (or steps) so that energy-sapping "blocks" are avoided. Although you temporarily avoid one unpleasant task by replacing it with a pleasant one, you discipline yourself to choose a pleasant one related to your overall goal. For example, you have to write up a report and you've reached a point where you find yourself putting it off and getting involved in distractions and less important things, like chatting with a co-worker or surfing the Internet. (Unfortunately some other "things," like starting another report, may generate more tasks, and related activities, that get you committed to tasks that you may, again, procrastinate about accomplishing.)

Instead of procrastinating by making a call to a friend—and not really enjoying the conversation because you feel guilty that you are procrastinating— you accomplish tasks related to your number one project. Let's say your report requires a bibliography. Instead of calling your friend when you are blocked on writing the report, you work on the report's bibliography. Another example: you have correspondence to do and you're procrastinating so at least you address the envelopes, or gather the necessary documentation to write the letters, rather than switch to an unrelated task.

Creative procrastination allows you to deviate from your ideal of working sequentially, from task to task, until you're done, but you will probably get the job done in the same, or even less, time. This method requires flexibility in your approach to your tasks (and it may not work in all situations), but for projects comprised of numerous steps it can help you to conquer a seeming insurmountable tendency to delay.

Solution #4 - Allow for delays.

Like all solutions you have to be careful that "allowing" yourself to procrastinate does not get out of hand so that you permanently avoid an unpleasant task. Sometimes just an hour, a day, or a week away from the task you are procrastinating about will provide the necessary energy, and motivation, to go forward with that task. (You may also find that an external motivation occurs to prompt you along: "The moving men are coming in two days" can inspire you to finish the packing you put off for two months.)

Procrastination may be tied to perfectionism in that you want, or need, to perform in a way that conforms to an unrealistic standard of excellence. Giving yourself permission to "goof off" or have a period of controlled procrastination may help you deal with this common problem without guilt or self-downing. "I'll call to cancel my reservation after I read this newspaper article" is more efficient than putting off the phone call, spending more time reminding yourself to do it than the time it will take to actually call.

You reap the benefits of licking procrastination, just as you pay the most for failing to overcome it. In some situations, however, delay is necessary or beneficial—e.g., planning something before doing it, completing your most important goal before your secondary ones. The trick is to know the difference between effective and self-indulgent procrastination.

Solution #5 - Don't let embarrassment exacerbate your procrastination.

The worst thing procrastinators can do is to abandon an important goal, or task, because they feel too embarrassed, discouraged, or guilty to finally tackle (and finish) a long-avoided activity. Usually "better late than never" is the adage to apply.

Paperwork

Anyone who deals with information, whether in an office or a hospital, is going to have paper to go through. Letters, memos, forms, reports, evaluations, meeting notices...the list goes on.

More will be discussed about paperwork in Chapter 6, *Improving Your Time at Work*. Another cause of paperwork that becomes overwhelming and messy clutter is failing to have systems to deal with the paperwork so that each type of incoming item, from letters and magazines to memos or upcoming meeting notices, is dealt with in a consistent way.

Solution #1 - Become ruthless about what you do with the paper in your office.

Make doing something about each piece of paper that comes across your desk a priority concern until you get your paperwork under control. Throw out, file, recycle, pass along, or scan each piece of paper into a master file so everything is in its place. If possible, avoid the temptation, or habit, of creating huge piles of paper (that may conceal the papers that are really important as well as requiring literally hours at a stretch to go through once it accumulates).

Solution #2 - Set aside regular time to sort through your paperwork.

Whether it is once a day, once a week, or even once a month, set aside time when you will sort through your paperwork. Include "paperwork" as part of your work or personal responsibilities, rather than seeing it as an annoyance that somehow you hope to "get through" once and for all.

Solution #3 - Have a system for dealing with each and every aspect of your daily mail and papers.

Promise yourself that you will go through your mail each day, putting the mail and other papers into the system you have created. (If you need help creating a system, see Chapter 6.)

The Terrible Twos: Telephone and Television

More will be said about these two notorious potential time gobblers later—the telephone in Chapter 6, and television in Chapter 8. For now, just start being aware of how much time you spend engaging in either activity, and what you should have—could have—been doing instead. Both are examples of habits which, uncontrolled, can eat up enormous amounts of time. Neither piece of equipment is in and of itself a bad habit; the frequency and duration of use determine its detrimental or beneficial effects.

Solution # 1 — Start a telephone or TV time log.

Begin keeping track of how long you spend engaged in either task, as well as what you are specifically watching or with whom you are speaking.

Start to note when you place calls; what you're doing when you receive calls (and if that effects how you deal with the caller); how long you usually stay on the phone, and who is the first to say "I have to go now."

Take stock of your television viewing as well, noting for starters if you watch specific programs or just have the TV on all the time. (As important as it is to stay abreast of current events, even watching the news all day long, if it is excessive and stopping you from doing your other work at hand, can be a time gobbler.)

Solution #2 — Designate a specific time to place or receive phone calls.

Instead of allowing calls to be put through constantly throughout your work day, pick out blocks of time when you will answer, or place, telephone calls. During the time when you prefer to do quiet creative work, or even have uninterrupted meetings, let your secretary screen calls or allow the voice mail or answering machine to take messages. If you wish to avoid telephone tag, you could also advise callers when to call back when it is more likely you will be there to take their call.

Solution #3 – Watch TV selectively.

Pick specific shows you will watch rather than having the TV on all the time. Excessive TV watching, if it is interfering with accomplishing work or leisure tasks that are more fundamental to your success and happiness, is as much of a bad habit as compulsive Internet use. Take control of the TV by observing just how much TV watching you are doing as well as the specific shows you want to view. (It also makes it easier to set an example for your children, whom you are probably trying to encourage to read, when they see their parents reading at night instead of watching too much TV.)

Solution #4 – Use a VCR to record your TV shows.

By recording your favorite programs using a VCR (video cassette recorder) you will have more control over when you watch TV. If you wish, you can also speed through commercials, spending only about 45 minutes watching an "hour" show.

Failure to prioritize

In addition to the solutions below, for help overcoming a failure to prioritize review the suggestions in the beginning of this chapter about solutions to overcome the "Doing Too Much at Once" syndrome as well as the advice for planning and goal setting in the previous chapter.

Solution # 1 – Be clear about your goals.

Having clear goals will help you prioritize (by saying "no" to anything that is not your #1 priority.)

Solution #2 – Take your time saying "yes."

If you at least take your time deciding to do something, you have a better chance of reminding yourself what your real priority is, and saying "no" to anything that distracts you.

Get comfortable saying these words, "I'll get back to you on that."

Commuting and Travel Time

Whether you spend two hours round trip each day commuting, or you work from home but spend four hours monthly on an airplane or an hour a day driving to work-related appointments, there's a lot of time at stake that is spent commuting daily or traveling for business.

There is a wide range in how this commuting or business travel time is utilized. Some flip through magazines, some read others' newspapers, some chat with a group of commuting friend regulars, some snore, and some stare into space, daydreaming or planning their day's activities.

What are some ways to make the most of travel time?

Solution # 1 – Have a commuting or travel time plan.

To creatively use your commuting or travel time: first, have a plan. Don't commute or travel aimlessly day after day, trip after trip. Based on how you commute, and how long it takes, decide if you will use your commuting time to do your work, for recreational activities, or for some combination of the two.

Solution #2 — Pick work-related tasks you can do while commuting or traveling for business.

If you commute alone by car there are safe, work-related tasks that you might consider, such as listening to work-related tapes or books on tape, known as audiobooks, available for sale or rental through bookstores, libraries, or special audiobook stores. You could also speak into a tape recorder to record your thoughts or letters for transcribing.

There are also numerous commercial and educational companies that sell prerecorded books that are ideal for commuters or travelers. (I often use driving time to listen to the monthly "audiomagazine" provided to busy members by the National Speakers Association, one of the associations I belong to.)

Solution # 2 – Bring along a portable or hand-held computer.

Having a portable computer could be a way for you to make maximum productive use of your commuting time. (Even if you do not have a portable or hand-held computer, you could still do your work the old-fashioned way, by taking along a pad and pencil or pen for writing; or magazines or books for work-related reading.)

Solution #3 – Use car commuting time for recreation and to reduce stress.

Listen to stress reduction music or tapes. But if you have a busy life, you might even find the silence while commuting alone a stress reducer of another sort. "I like the quiet," says a woman who commutes two hours a day alone in her car. "It gives me time to think," she adds, explaining how the rest of her day she's around people and scurrying between activities.

Although a car pool minimizes worrying about safety, it can introduce interruptions by other passengers. One van pool commuter, if she wants to read, and someone else wants to talk, answers whatever question or statement has been put to her, and immediately turns back to her reading, nipping a lengthy conversation before it starts.

Solution #4 – Exercise.

Productive use of commuting time by foot is, of course, the

utilization of that time for physical exercise. Walking to work is a way to combine exercise with your necessary commute.If you live within ten miles of your office, another possible option, if it is safe enough, is biking to work.

Solution #5 – Sleep.

Sometimes getting a nap on the train or plane is enough to replenish you for the workday (or leisure time) ahead. Of course you want to make sure you are awake before you reach your destination; you also want to be sure you keep your belongings safely concealed so nothing is stolen from you as you sleep.

Solution #6 - Socialize.

For some, the time spent in the car, on a train, bus, or plane talking with friends, co-workers, or even strangers adds welcome time for socializing to their workday.

Solution # 7 – Read.

You could use the commuting or business travel time to read for work or whatever you rarely seem to have the time to read — for example, the latest best-selling novel, a literary classic, a magazine about your hobby, poetry, or your child's latest school composition.

Solution # 8 – Daydream.

Not only is daydreaming relaxing, what you dream about just might offer you solutions to work-related problems you are trying to solve.

Solution # 9 - Meditate.

Meditating is known to reduce tension and stress.

Solution # 10 - Reconsider your long-term goals and your plans

to achieve them.

Use this commuting or business travel time to think about, or write about, your long term goals.

Solution # 11 - Take along stationery and catch up on your correspondence, or begin a personal journal.

Even though E-mail is replacing conventional correspondence in many instances, there are still times when an old-fashioned, handwritten note, or letter, is called for. Commuting or business travel time could provide just the opportunity for writing those letters or notes.

Solution #12 - Pick one obstacle to how you manage your time and map out a plan to overcome it.

Your commuting or business travel time could offer you the opportunity to work on your number one time management obstacle.

Solution #13 - Use commuting or business travel time to do errands or chores.

To or from work you could do chores or errands. Business travel time could provide the time and opportunity for buying holiday or birthday presents.

Complaining

How often have you uttered a complaint, and immediately wished you hadn't? Our culture sanctions silent stoicism, with phrases like "stiff upper lip," and "never complain, never explain."Yet, the act of complaining is natural, and quite prevalent. Its legitimacy is judged by: what you gripe about; to whom you bleat; and how often you grumble.

These three criteria interrelate; together, they determine whether a statement is deemed an observation, a self-pitying complaint, or a time waster. For example, getting your gripes off your chest once in a while might help you break through your delaying tactics. Complaining might provide you with information; e.g., you complain to a coworker about the deadline pressures you feel and she tells you the proposal isn't due for another month.

By and large, chronic complaining wastes time that could be spent thinking and doing. Complaints can bring strangers and intimates closer—or send them running for cover. Hilda, 68, a retired librarian, says, "Complaining is probably good for the person who complains, and awful for everyone else around."

Complaining may be a way to gain sympathy or control in a situation. Example: "I worked like a dog today. Stuck in traffic for two hours, trying to fix equipment for five hours, and you think you have problems?" The man who said that to his wife did not want to listen to her. His complaints may be his way of justifying his demand she spend her time catering to his needs.

Solution #1 - Deal with the source of your complaining.

If your complaint is about a specific person—and you can't go forward until your differences are resolved—a face-to-face confrontation might be the most efficient way to handle things. If that is unrealistic, writing a long letter—one that you might ultimately decide would be best not mailed—can "get it all out" and help you go on with the business at hand. (A daily journal serves the same purpose, but on an ongoing basis.)

Solution #2 - Recognize the potential career consequences to complaining.

Complaining not only wastes your own time, but also creates a very poor image of what you're like—people will welcome your sympathy yet will make a mental note that you cannot be relied on for "positive thinking." You may find the label "gloomy" a difficult one to live down.

Solution # 3 —Put things in perspective.

Listen more to what others say and you may realize your complaints are petty. Read some inspirational books, like Harold S. Kushner's *When Bad Things Happen to Good People* or Viktor E. Frankl's *Man's Search for Meaning,* and consider ways other than complaining that you might try to get through life's disappointments. A thirty-year-old bachelor, for example, does volunteer work with terminally ill cancer patients rather than complaining about his own loneliness. Accent the positive in life, and be more realistic in expectations, so you'll have less to complain about. One chronic complainer confesses, "Even if I go beyond my goals I am still not satisfied."

Solution #4 — Find other things to talk about.

Ask yourself: Do I complain because I have nothing else to say? If you answer "yes," read about compulsive talking in this book.

Solution #5 — Find other ways to get attention.

Do you complain to get attention? If so, find more effective attention-getting mechanisms, such as increasing your knowledge in a certain area so you have more to say, or looking more attractive. Plan, and execute, actions that may correct specific complaints that now preoccupy you. Speak your complaints into a tape recorder and force yourself to listen to the tape, as if you were the coworker, friend, or spouse who might have to listen to you. If all else fails, complain to taxi drivers, bartenders, or therapists who expect to hear complaints as part of their job.

Excuses

An occasional excuse, when valid, because a completely unexpected event occurs that necessitates a change in your plans, is simply part of life. For example, you would have gotten to work on time but you had an unexpected car emergency and had to bring your car to the service station on your way to work. But when excuses become chronic, and a too easy way to cover up poor planning, procrastination, or an inability to prioritize, you have to look at the pattern of excuses, and the consequences, and stop yourself from making excuses.

Solution #1 — Keep track of your excuses by writing them down.

You may be unaware of how often you use an excuse to put off doing what you have to do. By writing down your excuses, you will become more aware of this habit, as well as having evidence of exactly what excuses you are using. This could help you see what pattern your excuses fall into, and how to get out of using excuses as a way of sabotaging yourself and stopping yourself from better time management (and greater success).

Solution #2— Try to figure out what is behind each excuse.

Look at the excuses you have written down. Is there a pattern to your excuses? Are you always blaming someone else for your shortcomings? Are you always using something you have no control over, like the weather, to justify your actions (which you do have control over)?

The next chapter will discuss emotional blocks to time management such as fear or failure and fear of success.

4
Emotional Blocks to Time Management

Time is flying, never to return.
VIRGIL, *Georgics III*

Consider the emotional blocks to time management discussed in this chapter. It will help to recognize, and overcome, each one that might be blocking your effective and creative time management.

Perfectionism

The perfectionist is never pleased and, sometimes without knowing it, belabors assignments beyond what is required for a best effort, and reworks things past deadlines (if they finish at all). Perfectionism is a difficult habit to break because it means rethinking one's entire approach to how one appraises people, things, and events.

We all need ideals to aspire to, but when the ideal becomes a day-to-day unrealistic and unattainable goal, frustration and poor time management may result. Why try at all if your efforts will never satisfy you or anyone else? or so thinks the perfectionist.

The perfectionist never finishes a report, or misses deadline after deadline, because there's always "just one more" reference to read. A new product is revised so often, far beyond what is needed, that the competition is able to launch theirs first, enjoying all the atttention and profits that could have been the perfectionist's.

On a personal level, sometimes those who are overweight are really perfectionists about their appearance. Overweight, they can fantasize about how perfect they'd be if they lost weight. Sometimes those who look for the "perfect" mate fail to find a mate at all.

Perfectionism camouflages fear of failure and of success. Someone is so afraid of failing that he or she set standards inappropriate to the task—for example, spending four days over a one paragraph letter that has to be written, writing and rewriting beyond realistic standards of excellence. Or you are so (unwittingly) afraid of succeeding that you convince yourself your letter is *still* not good enough so you never send it or you send it thinking you could have—should have—done better.

Perfectionists have a low self-image concealed behind their "I know what's right" facade. Perfectionism is a character trait that interferes with effective use of your time. It causes mismanaged time; strive for excellence, not unattainable perfection.

Solution #1 – Recognize that you are a perfectionist.

The first cure for perfectionism is realizing that you even have this problem in the first place. Once you realize you are a perfectionist, you can begin to recognize when you're defeating yourself by setting unrealistic, unattainable goals, which are out of reach. Are you a perfectionist? You may not be a perfectionist about everything, just certain things. You may be a perfectionist about others, always finding fault and wishing they dressed, spoke, acted, or went about their lives in a different ("perfect") way.

Solution #2 — Accept that no one, including you, is perfect, and learn to feel comfortable by praise.

Embrace and accept yourself for what you are, with all your failings and imperfections. Develop more realistic assessments of yourself, others, and situations. (This change in attitude, however, should not become a way of excusing sloppiness or behavior that is unacceptable.)

If your perfectionism is a way of preventing yourself from feeling good about yourself or what you do, learn to feel comfortable being complimented.

Solution #3 – Learn to pursue attainable excellence, rather than unattainable perfectionist standards.

What you want to do, if you have this trait in one or more areas, is to turn your perfectionism into high but more manageable and realistic standards that are *attainable* by you. By becoming more realistic in your expectations, perfectionism can be channeled into high, but attainable, standards.

Solution #4 — Delegate.

Another possible solution for the perfectionist is to delegate authority. By accepting that someone can do certain jobs for you, perhaps not exactly the way you would do it but as well as the task requires—you will free up valuable time and energy for other pursuits. The time you save by having a research assistant find and order the latest books on a topic or having an intern or a secretary screen your telephone calls may help you to devote more time to your priority tasks as well as providing you with more leisure time. By welcoming the help of others – and recognizing that they can assist you in completing some of your tasks and that they can do that work adequately – will help you to overcome the perfectionism that has probably caused you to feel only you can do your work.

Becoming more accepting of the strengths, and weaknesses, of others is the first step toward a more relaxed approach to yourself and to your work.

By delegating to others, you will learn to become more flexible (and less of a perfectionist) by accepting that there are more than two ways to do something (your way, and the wrong way.)

Solution #5 — Be aware of the consequences of perfectionism.

Another solution to perfectionism is to become aware of what you miss out on because of your perfectionism. It may, interestingly, be in only one or a few areas that you, or someone you know, is a perfectionist. Parents may have such unrealistic standards for their children that their offspring can never please them (or themselves). You miss out on enjoying what you or others *are* accomplishing as well as on reality by focusing on perfectionist fantasies.

Fear of Failure

If you don't try, you can't fail, or so thinks the person with a fear of failure. But by working at a level far below your potential, or by never finishing a major project that you could be judged by, you may bring on the very failure you fear since you may not give your all, whether to a project, a relationship, or a job.

Here are some suggestions for overcoming a fear of failure:

Solution #1 – Get adequate training and experience.

Confidence, which reduces a fear of failure, comes from competence and accomplishment. A fear of failure may be reduced or eliminated by doing all that you can to insure your success.

Solution #2 - Change your attitude toward failure.

Another way to conquer your fear of failure is to reevalute how you view it. Making mistakes (failures) has a negative connotation in our culture; we applaud achievement and push thwarted relationships or projects under the rug. Without those "failures," (it's better to call them "efforts"), there could be no successes. Susan, 34, an actress who has had more jobs as a waitress than parts in plays, describes her fear of failing as an actress:

I wonder if all the time that I thought I was good, and thought I was talented, maybe it wasn't really true. That would mean that I would have to change my whole life, change my career. I would have to have a whole new life, and that's very frightening.

Once Susan, and others who fear failure, analyze the situation that they fear, they may open up new options (and opportunities) for success. This is how management consultant Peter F. Drucker views failure. Writing in *The Practice of Management*, he states:

> Nobody learns except by making mistakes. The better a man is the more mistakes he will make—for the more new things he will try. I would never promote a man into a top-level job who has not made mistakes, and big ones at that. Otherwise he is sure to be mediocre. Worse still, not having made mistakes he will not have learned how to spot them early and how to correct them.

Failure itself is usually not fatal; fearing it can put a negative spin on all your efforts, even narrowing your initial vision so you stop yourself from striving for the goals you really want to achieve.

Solution #3 — Imagine the worst consequence of what you're doing, and see yourself surviving that situation.

Another way to cope with a fear of failure is to imagine the worst consequences of what you are doing. Take the failure you fear and fantasize it to the extreme. Example: you overcome your fear of failure and give up your middle management job to go back to school and become an accountant. You graduate, become licensed, but cannot get a job. Or you cannot get clients. Or you decide, after all that, that you really liked the job you left better than your new goal. Ask yourself: Can you live with that? Could you still view the years of study as useful even if you return to your old job?

By imagining the worst that might happen, and picturing yourself overcoming that failure, you can go on to try to achieve the goals that you fear.

Solution #4 — View failure as a training ground.

Fear of failure is tied very closely to fear of success. The solution for a fear of failure is similar to the solution for a fear of success: do your best but if you fail, learn what you can from what you did (or did not) do. Each experience increases your ability to withstand further failures (mistakes) and to achieve even more successes.

Solution #5 — Be realistic about the causes of your failure; take responsibility for your part in it.

If you find yourself blaming everyone else or circumstances "beyond your control" each time you fail, your fear of failure may be causing you to mismanage your time by avoiding responsibility. Objective self-evaluation, unlike "if only" fantasies, saves time by using mistakes creatively for self-advancement.

Fear of Success

No one wants to fail, and everyone wants to succeed, right? Wrong. According to psychologist Leon Tec and others, a fear of success is quite common. In *Fear of Success,* Tec writes:

> I believe the fear of success is universal, so widespread that it must be considered normal. It may be severe in some people, less intense in others, but it is always there. Even for those who ostensibly have succeeded and reached the top of their fields, the fear of success may exist and rob them of the enjoyment of their feats.

Here are recommendations for coping with this time waster:

Solution #1 — Fantasize about success and imagine yourself dealing with all the consequences of it.

Take a few moments to fantasize about what would happen if you were successful—really successful—in either your professional or personal life. Would friends or relatives be jealous? What would you do differently? Would you squander your fortune, or become addicted to drugs? Would the old gang feel you're not one of them any more? Would you become depressed because you would have nothing left to strive for? Strange as it sounds, some people grow used to being unhappy—or poor or fat or lonely. Susan, the struggling actress, says, "There's something secure in staying where you are, no matter how bad it is, rather than going into something else, unknown ground."

Try this to face up to your fear of success: imagine the best that could happen—and all the negative consequences that might follow—and see yourself coping with that. Picture yourself coping with the joys success will bring, as well as the disappointments.

Solution #2 — Analyze how realistic you are about what success means.

Ask yourself how realistic your images of success are. Is it all rosy and wonderful? If you fantasize success as only positive you may be afraid to succeed and test out your unrealistic expectations. Consider that success may mean that you, and everyone else, may expect more from you in the future. You may be afraid of the good, and bad, changes that success will necessitate. Is success your "if only. . ." one-note song that camouflages deep-seated insecurity? Are your standards so high, and so unrealistic, that you are successful, and you don't even know it? Thus you may have to become more realistic about what success means—at work and in personal relationships— to discover if you have achieved it and, if not, how to go about getting it.

Devaluing (or Overvaluing) of Your Activities

For some, it's difficult to believe—and live up to the belief—that what you do matters. "In the end it doesn't really matter what you do," says a man with low self-esteem. There are also those who are so self-important that they think their every deed is momentous. ("Look at me," they seem to be saying, as if the whole world is one big parent whose love they are trying to win.) Then there are those who waver back and forth between these two extremes— either what they do is the best or the worst, very important or meaningless.

Dealing with life realistically means operating somewhere in the middle of these extremes. It is a waste of time to be either a minimizer or a maximizer; both are distorted views of events and persons. It's also unrealistic to expect everyone around you to match your own natural intense self-interest.

Solution #1 — Develop standards that are more realistic and objective.

A solution to devaluing, or overvaluing, your work or personal activities is to honestly appraise your past efforts, your current time demands, and your future goals. Are your paintings good enough to show in a gallery? If not, are they still first-rate as a hobby? Is the report you wrote terrific, or just " so-so," and not something you should be bragging about? As a friend used to say, when asked what she thought about a new date, "Good, not great." Most efforts fall into the "good, not great" category. Perceiving everything you do as worthless or, the opposite extreme, brilliant, mismanages your time.

Solution #2 —Work on your self-esteem so you need not be a self-downer nor someone who always has to "one-up" everyone.

When I give writing seminars, my students – the typical eighteen-year-old college student as well as the fifty-year-old full-time employee or the seventy-five-year-old retiree who is looking to writing as a second or fifth career – are comforted when I say "You can still get your writing published even if you are a good but not a great writer. There's still a need for writers who are good but not as brilliant as Hemingway or F. Scott Fitzgerald."

For some, that more realistic self-assessment of their writing helps them to overcome writer's block – or the selling block – that is preventing them from completing their magazine or book projects and finally getting their writing published.

Impatience and Low Frustration Tolerance

Are you impatient? Impatience prevents optimal use of your time. Examples: you're so eager to complete one phone call, and get on to the next, that you fail to be a good listener or to remember much of what was said. You send someone a non-urgent E-mail asking for some information for your own personal use. Instead of waiting for a reply, a few days later you call, further annoying the busy person who had planned, in good time, to respond to you.

Difficulty in handling frustration is related to impatience. That wastes time because your energy is spent fuming at problems—not solving them. Both of these "I want it *now*" personality traits are time wasters in the same way that perfectionism wastes time. Impatience may cause you to give up before you have expended the time and effort needed for the task at hand; perfectionism may cause you to continually redo or prolong a task too long because your standards are too high and unattainable.

Those who are impatient, and have low frustration tolerance, are filled with self-loathing, since they give up too quickly to see the results that they crave. Those who are perfectionists are usually too hard on themselves (and others) and won't give up even when they have done as much as is necessary or feasible.

Impatience and low frustration tolerance is symptomatic of immaturity and a need for immediate gratification. Yet many of the greatest rewards in how we spend our time at work or in our personal lives are for accomplishing little steps and continuing on a path even when frustrated. Curing impatience and low frustration tolerance means becoming process, as well as product, oriented. You may want to appear on national TV hyping your best-selling book, but you first need to find ongoing rewards in the day-to-day efforts necessary to achieve the first step of writing the book.

Solution #1 — Work on this problem, one task at a time.

Like other time wasters, retraining yourself to be more patient, and to have a higher frustration tolerance, in one area of your life may help you to successfully apply it, step by step, to other areas as well.

Pick just one task you have to complete, or just one bad habit that you want to change, and force yourself to stick with your goal in spite of impatience or low frustration tolerance. That specific instance of conquering impatience may help you to generalize your overall approach to your activities and relationships.

Solution #2 — Count to ten.

The next time something happens that demonstrates that you are impatient or that you have a low frustration tolerance—the photocopy machine breaks down and you want to scream at the machine, a secretary, or anyone nearby who will listen— decide that you have the self-control necessary to handle that frustrating situation in a more patient, mature way. Count to ten. Walk away from the situation and come back once you have regained control. Practicing patience is reinforcing.

Solution #3 — Tackle impatience and low frustration tolerance as if it's a phobia you are trying to overcome.

Look at impatience and low frustration tolerance as phobias and cure those tendencies in the way you would treat a phobic response to, let's say, an elevator. In that case, you would get in the elevator and wouldn't close the doors. Mastering that, you would then ride to the fourth floor. In time, you would be able to still feel comfortable riding to the top of the World Trade Center. In a similiar way, gradually increase your tolerance to frustration.

Solution #4 — Become more patient with others or in delays that are unavoidable.

You may have to learn to handle others more patiently if you are to handle your own time (and impatience) more effectively. Even if you think you can do something faster or better, than someone – everyone – else, you need to be patient with the pace that others are able to handle. Sometimes you may need to tolerate that others have a slower pace, even if that is not the pace you comfortably perform at. By accepting the behavior – or pace – of others, you may become more patient in general.

If you believe in the path you have chosen, even if it means being patient about monetary or other gratifications, it may require convincing yourself or those around to be more patient to avoid wasting time focusing on what cannot be rushed.

Jealousy

Jealousy squanders time because it fosters downing others (and yourself) instead of doing whatever it takes to get what you want.

Learn to recognize jealousy in yourself and in others even when it is disguised. "I don't care if she makes seventy-five thousand dollars, she'll still be miserable" or "It's because of sheer luck that he's gotten where he is" are wet-blanket statements that attempt to diminish an accomplishment (and perpetuate the jealousy of the speaker).

You cannot stop others from being jealous of you, although you may wish to reevaluate why you seem to surround yourself with jealous people. You can, however, learn to understand, and minimize, the jealousy that you feel, and that wastes your time.

Solution #1 — Turn jealousy into something useful and positive.

A solution for your own time-sapping jealousy is to turn it into something effective and productive. Jealousy pinpoints what you value, since the rage and envy you feel when someone else achieves something clarifies what you want for yourself. Turn your jealousy into a fact-finding expedition; find out how someone else did what he or she did and try to learn from his or her example how *you* can do it too.

Put your fantasies of "if only" to the test and see if there is information to be gained that would save you time, and help you to achieve what you really want.

Solution #2 — Build your self-esteem.

Become secure enough within yourself that you do not need to diminish others through feeling, or expressing, jealousy. Take the time and energy that you used to spend being jealous and work at achieving what you want, whether that is wealth, fame, popularity, confidence, a nicer disposition, greater productivity, or whatever your goal or pleasure.

The Inability to Take Criticism

The inability to take criticism is an incredible time waster since it may lead to abandoning a project because one small part has to be changed, to counterproductive self-hate, and to poor relationships, since those who are unable to take criticism often blame, and may actually hate, the ones who criticize them. You have to learn how to deal with criticism in an objective way if you are to make better use of your time.

"Sometimes I can feel so devastated by criticism that I feel that I want to give up acting," says Susan, the aspiring actress who also has a fear of failure. Interestingly, Susan is only "devastated" if the criticism is from someone she "respects." "Some people I just don't respect," she says, "so the criticism means absolutely nothing to me, and I think I know better than they do, so I don't listen to it." Your inability to take criticism may be so all pervasive, however, that it devastates you no matter who is doing the criticizing, or what it is about.

Psychologist Lynn Diamond gives this explanation for the inability to take criticism:

Nobody wants to fail. It's rejection. The fear of failure, or the fear of being rejected, is very great in all of us.... [But] it has nothing to do with you and your project. You are not your product. You could be totally acceptable, but I may not like your writing. The whole goal of acceptance is to set a standard for your performance. "This report was good and I'd like you to change x" doesn't mean that you failed. It means you can do things to get better.

Solution #1 – Create conditions that make it easier to accept the criticism.

The following conditions make it easier to take criticism; try to achieve them in your work and personal situations
- People know your work.
- They already respect your abilities.
- They like you.
- They are trying to help you to improve (yourself or your product).

You have to learn to distinguish whether you are dealing with a knowledgeable, and critical, person who is providing beneficial advice, or with a sadistic and "always right" person who can never be pleased.

Solution #2 — Develop your ability to accept (and give) criticism.

If you are unable to take criticism, and you seek out only those who approve and praise you, in the long run you may waste time since you, and your work, may not improve.

In the business classic, *One Minute Manager,* co-authors Blanchard and Johnson expressed this idea quite simply: the key to success is one minute praising *and* one minute reprimands.

Usually the person who is unable to take criticism is also uncomfortable being critical. That's the kind of person who says you look great even when you look terrible.

To work on your inability to take criticism, learn how to give it. If you feel secure, you will be able to discriminate about the criticism that is offered, neither blindly accepting nor blindly rejecting it.

Solution #3 — Redefine how you view criticism.

Look at criticism as observations, rather than judgments, and be objective about it. Is the criticism valid? If it is valid, how will you go about improving whatever has been criticized—the report, your appearance, the time you spend on the Internet or the phone, how you handle meetings? If it is invalid, how can you explain to your criticizer that his comment is unwarranted?

Solution #5 — Self-evaluate so outside criticism occurs less often.

Maintain such high standards of self-evaluation that criticism is an infrequent occurrence.

Solution #6 - Stop automatically defending yourself.

If a criticism might have merit, be open to it rather than automatically defending yourself. If you are uncomfortable thanking someone for a criticism, try to at least say, "I'll consider your comments."

Boredom

Call it blahs, ennui, or tedium, boredom is that "ho-hum" feeling when the meeting is dull, or you have to do the same thing too often. There are discernible trends to boredom. For example, some are able to keep themselves interested outside of work, but are bored at their job. Others, who thrive on their work, are bored in their leisure time. Some are chronically bored; others feel boredom only when they are stressed, insecure, or doing a repetitious task.

How does boredom interfere with effective management of your time? Boredom lends to unproductive activities, or shifting gears in the hope of curing boredom; beginnings are often more exciting than middles so it leads to the "doing too many things at once" syndrome. In the end, however, more time is lost since it is usually more efficient to stick with one thing till it is completed before starting on numerous new things.

Solution #1 - Change the task.

If your boredom is caused by doing too much of the same thing, change the task. For example, if you're tired of writing letters, make a phone call to contact someone; if you are bored returning e-mail, write a letter instead.

Solution #2 — Do the same thing, in a different way.

If you need to finish a task, but are bored, try doing the same task differently. For example, if you are bored writing letters on a computer, try writing a few notes in longhand. If you are tired responding to E-mails, try calling someone on the phone or sending him or her a fax. If you are tired writing a report on your computer at your desk, try taking a draft of the report to a nearby conference room or a coffee shop, where you continue to work on it.

Solution #3 — Change the order of the tasks you have to accomplish.

Consider doing something else first, like running, reading the newspaper, or screening a film, before launching into a boring task (or a task that was initially interesting but has become boring).

Solution #4 – Try the reward system (that is also useful in overcoming procrastination).

Promise yourself a reward for completing a necessary, but boring, activity. "If I finish addressing all these envelopes, I will read that article in the trade journal that peaked my interest." "If I return these last two phone calls, I will get back to writing the report and stay off the phone for at least an hour."

Solution #5 — Become more sensitive to your moods.

Another way to offset the inertia when boredom strikes is to become sensitive to your moods, and then use your moods to save time. For example, if you are feeling "up," tackle boring tasks that might take longer if you are feeling tired or depressed. If you are a "morning" person, do your most creative work when you first get to work. Save the correspondence for after lunch, when you are slower anyway, so you will be less resentful of being bored since you already accomplished your priority tasks for the day.

Solution #6 — Look at the causes of your boredom as a source of solutions for overcoming it.

If your boredom is caused by too much work, or poor planning, you can cure it by getting more rest, relaxing, exercising, or saying "No, sorry. Thanks anyway for asking."

Consider if your boredom actually has a more obscure cause: you took on such an overwhelming task that it is a camouflage for the feeling of fatigue or befuddlement.

Reconsider the frequency of a task as a possible reason for boredom: one progress report a month is useful, once a week might be better, but daily reports might become boring and unproductive.

Solution #7 — Recognize that some boredom is beneficial.

Too much boredom certainly wastes time, but some ennui has value. "I keep busy every minute because I never want to be bored," says a married man with a toddler who works two demanding jobs. "There's no monotony in what I do, and every task is different.

Maybe a little boredom might prove restful," he adds, breathlessly.

Solution #8 — On careful analysis, consider boredom a symptom that you should be delegating certain tasks.

Boredom may be a symptom that you are working so far below your potential and capacities that you are dulled. In that case, see boredom as a sign that you should be delegating those tasks to others who either would not be bored or would welcome doing those particular activities for the experience, the pay check, or a distraction from their own work which is either overwhelming or boring them. (For more information on delegating, see the delegating section in Chapter 6, *Improving Your Time at Work*.)

Guilt

Are you the kind of person who feels guilty about what you *are* doing as well as by what you're *not* doing? Do you feel guilty for working late, because you're neglecting your family, and guilty if you leave work on time, since your work is being put aside?

Most people waste time and energy with minor everyday guilts, like not returning a phone call that could certainly wait till tomorrow, postponing a meeting because something else came up that had to be dealt with immediately. (Note: this section is not about major guilts, like criminal behavior or falsifying a resume, actions that *should* cause guilt.)

How does guilt waste time? Because the guilt itself starts to consume time as the guilty person ruminates, time that could be spent more productively on work or leisure pursuits.

If guilt wastes your time, consider its source. "Most of the guilt I feel stems from my parent's voice, which is something I hear in my head," a guilt-ridden college student says.

Solution #1 – Try to recognize the source of your guilt.

Next time you feel guilty, try to recognize the guilt-provoking voice you are hearing. Is it your father? Mother? Teacher? By recalling that voice and thinking "I hear you, but I refuse to feel guilty"— you're on the road toward a less guilty life.

Solution #2 – Clarify your values, priorities, and beliefs.

Guilt stems from trying to please others, rather than yourself. If you establish your own fair guidelines, you won't blow with the breeze of outside (guilt-provoking) pressure from others.

Solution #3 – Allow yourself to make mistakes.

Stop ruminating over past errors. Learn from current or past mistakes and make notes about what happened and why, but stop beating yourself up over it.

Solution #4 – Remind yourself about what you can and cannot control, and recognize the difference.

You are not to blame for your boss's bad mood, or the decision to relocate your firm. You are not responsible for others, only for yourself, although others may choose to behave in a certain way because of your actions.

Solution #5 – Lower your expectations.

If your expectations are completely unattainable, you are setting yourself up to feel guilty if you fail, even if your standard was impractical. If your goals are unrealistic, adjust them. Try for very good, so if you get excellent, you come out ahead.

Selflessness

For most of us, selfishness has a negative connotation. To philosopher and novelist Ayn Rand, author of *The Virtue of Selfishness: A New Concept of Egoism*, it meant, simply "concern for one's own interests."

Using Rand's neutral definition, the inability to be selfish (selflessness) wastes time because you spend too much of your precious time meeting others' demands. Furthermore, selflessness violates a basic time management principle since you cannot prioritize if self-interests are considered last, if at all.

The inability to be selfish is tied to another time waster, the inability to say "no"—you take on too many commitments for fear of alienating someone, or of losing that opportunity forever.

Till recently, selflessness seemed to afflict women more than men. Women, socialized to put others first, became martyrs. Donna Goldfein, President and founder of ESTE (Easy Steps Toward Efficiency) based in San Francisco, conducts seminars for women; she encourages them to find time for their own priorities. "Women, especially women over thirty, still have a guilt about being selfish," Goldfein explains. How does Goldfein help them to change? "They learn not to live vicariously through others, but to do something for themselves."

The inability to be selfish, however, afflicts men as well. "I often assume the title of 'Mr. Nice Guy,'" says a store manager. "Although this is a personality boost for me, once I start helping others, it's expected. As soon as I slack off, I'm labeled a lazy slob."

Although you need not feel guilty about saying "no" when you are selfless—because you are always saying "yes"—it wastes time because your own goals are ignored or postponed. Resentments may build, reaching a point where you explode, flee, or waste more time than if you had appropriately practiced the right amount of selfishness all along.

If selflessness is wasting too much of your time, here are some solutions for overcoming this tendency:

Solution #1 - See selfishness as a positive trait.

Selfishness reaffirms your priorities by forcing you to say, "This is the #1 concern in my life right now. I will attend to this, or to this person, before everything or everyone else."

If being selfish is an uncomfortable concept for you, try substituting the word *self-interested*. Try saying the word without choking up. "I am self-interested and that is good." Those with healthy self-interest get ahead and succeed; those who are overly selfless often become resentful doormats.

Solution #2 – Reevaluate the demands that others are placing on you.

Which ones are reasonable? Which ones are shifting too much of the work unfairly to you? Learn to say "no" to unfair or excessive requests.

Realize that being selfish is not like being self-absorbed or narcissistic. Selfishness means a balanced system of exchange: you neither get, nor give, too much. If your boss gives you ten clients, and your co-workers have only six, unless you're working on commission, you've lightened their load, at your own expense.

Solution #3 – Equate some selfishness with self-actualizing.

To overcome excessive selflessness, see the right amount of self-interest or selfishness as being self-actualizing because, in moderation, that's what it is. Self-actualizing people are better time managers because they value and wisely guard their time.

Being in Love, and Other Emotional Issues

Take the case of one executive, who was taking three-hour lunches since learning his wife was cheating on him. Or the administrative assistant, whose productivity in the last year has been less than half of what it used to be when her romantic relationship was going well. Or the bride and groom who find phone calls about their upcoming wedding as well as shopping trips and fittings are eating into their workday productivity.

Perhaps you've been upset lately but you thought you would

be able to pull yourself together over a three-day weekend or certainly during your annual two weeks off. Yet you are back at work, still preoccupied with your problems.

Here are some symptoms that your personal problems are affecting your work performance:

- Your concentration is poor.
- Your sense of time is distorted; the hours drag on.
- Your personal problems preoccupy you at work.
- You begin to "look" busy while you're working, but you are only shuffling papers and not accomplishing anything.
- You personalize everything that happens. ("He doesn't like my report because he's trying to undermine my success." "She put through that call because she's angry at me today.")

The most typical solution —trying to solve your emotional crises by talking it out at work—is probably the least effective and riskiest to your career. Yet many workers, seeking quick solutions for their problems or needing to share, ask colleagues, employers, or even bosses for sympathy or advice. Yet the competitive world of work is rarely if ever the place to parade your personal problems.

Should you tell your boss the reason your productivity is lower? Use your discretion and instincts to make that decision.

Here are some solutions to consider if being in love or other emotional issues are causing you to mismanage your time:

Solution #1 — Evaluate your work performance: are you coping well on your own?

Evaluate your current productivity and ask yourself if personal, romantic, or familial situations are affecting how you manage your work time. If you are being productive, no one, including you, should have to consider this issue any further. But if being in love or personal or familial problems are preventing you from doing your best, you have some decisions to make.

Your goal is to solve your problems, of course, but, along the way, you have to do well enough at your job that you don't lose it while you put your affairs back in order.

Solution #2 – Realize that most emotional crises will impact on your productivity, so cut yourself some slack.

Certain types of emotional crises, such as dealing with the death of a loved one, being the victim of a major crime, divorce, or coping with a major illness (your own or a family member's), may cause someone to go through one or all of the stages first described by psychiatrist Kubler-Ross from her work with the terminally ill and their immediate families: shock, denial, disbelief, fright and fear, clinging behavior, apathy alternating with anger, and, finally, resolution. (These stages are also described in greater detail as related to crime victims in Martin Symonds's journal article on crime victims as well as in my own book, *Victims*.)

Since your productivity may be impacted by such major emotional crises, lower your expectations for yourself till you are able to get back to your "old self." If possible, revise deadlines that could be adjusted; delegate whatever you can while still maintaining quality control during this adjustment time.

Solution #3 — Consider finding outside assistance to help you cope.

If you are bringing your problems to work, or it is impacting on your productivity, consider getting help from an individual, family, or marital therapist. Consider short- or long-term therapy. Short-term therapy of three to five sessions is usually directed at a specific situation: "Here's what happened to me. Here's what I want to be able to do. Can you help me?" However, it is only upon consultation with a therapist that you will be able to make the determination if short-term, long-term, or even drug-assisted therapy is needed.

Solution #4 — Consider other sources of help as well.

Not everyone needs outside professional help to cope with personal problems. A support network of friends and family members is invaluable in getting you through a crisis without inappropriately relying on coworkers, subordinates, superiors, or clients.

Support groups might be another source of help. If there has been a death in the family, or of a close friend or even a pet, you might want to consider attending a local support group for the bereaved. Today there are support groups – run by the members or run by a professional therapist – for almost every personal, professional, or medical crisis as well as for the family or friends of those going through such crises, such as coping with cancer, job loss, eating disorders, caring for an elderly parent, and so forth. (For an extensive list of self-help groups, see *The Self-Help Sourcebook* compiled by Barbara J. White and Edward J. Madara through the American Self-Help Clearinghouse.)

Solution #5 — Take some time off.

Perhaps for you just getting some time off from work, or taking a vacation, will help you to resolve your emotional conflicts.

Should you tell those you work with the real reason you need time off? Use your judgment although some experts point out that physical complaints ("I'm not feeling well") may be more acceptable, and carry less of a stigma, than tales of emotional duress.

Solution #5 — Get better separating work and personal roles.

Work at keeping your personal life out of the workplace so you can function effectively at work despite your emotional crises. It's easier said than done but sometimes work actually takes your mind off your problems, if you let yourself get absorbed in your work.

Here's another spin on this issue: Your emotional life may be fine but if you chronically bring problems home from the office, you may be creating a different personal problem that needs to be solved. By letting too much of your work concerns spill over into your personal or family time, you may find your dutiful listeners tuning you out, asking you to switch the subject, or being forced to avoid you if the problem becomes serious enough.

Somehow—on your own, with the aid of friends or family, or with the help of a therapist or a support group—you have to find a way to keep work at work so you do not create personal problems (that will, in turn, begin to impact on your work productivity). Apply solutions 1 through 5 to this different spin on the same problem – namely, you are in love with your work and that over-emphasis on work is causing problems in your romantic or family life.

Refer back to the section in Chapter 3 on complaining (pages 27-29), and concentrate your efforts on improving the faulty situation. You could also refer to the sections in this book on workaholism since often this is a symptom of the workaholic, someone whose life has become disproportionately focused on work to the detriment of others.

Bad Habits

Fortunately, with some effort, time-saving habits can replace time-wasting ones. Whether the time-saving techniques that you wish to adopt are major, like becoming organized rather than disorganized, or minor, they will become habits only if they are consistently applied. You may make more money because of these new, positive habits, or get praise from your family or friends, but, even more importantly, your life will be more orderly and relaxed.

If you procrastinate, or do too many things at once, you will have to make an active effort to change if you want to manage your time more effectively. The only way to change is to make a conscious—and daily—effort in that direction. In *How People Change*, psychologist Alan Wheelis points out: "Personality change follows change in behavior. Since we are what we do, if we want to change what we are we must begin by changing what we do, must undertake a new mode of action."

Initially, however, you may not be thrilled by your new, improved habits. Face the fact that for some, in the beginning, even beneficial changes may make you irritable, disagreeable, cranky, and less efficient. As Wheelis notes: "The new mode will be experienced as difficult, unpleasant, forced, unnatural, anxiety provoking. It may be undertaken lightly but can be sustained only by considerable effort of will. Change will occur only if such action is maintained over a long period of time."

Changing—and coping successfully with new situations—necessitates being in touch with who you are, and what you want. To embrace change means to be secure and self-determined. If you are thrown by change—new and unforeseen circumstances—you may also be reluctant to give up changing yourself and your bad habits, however ineffective and self-sabotaging they are.

In *What Life Should Mean to You*, psychologist Alfred Adler writes about change:

> If we see emotions that apparently cause difficulties and run counter to the individual's own welfare, it is completely useless to begin by trying to change these emotions. They are the right expression of the individual's style of life, and they can be uprooted only if he changes his style of life.

There are entire books you can read on how to change bad habits, but here, in a nutshell, are several possible solutions:

Solution #1 — First decide exactly what *you* want to change about yourself.

Do not blindly accept others' pronouncements for you; your procrastination may be a bad habit, or it may be purposeful and time effective. Focusing your attention on a specific bad habit that *you* want to change will augment your motivation to change it.

Solution #2 — Work on changing just one habit at a time.

If you try to change too many habits at once, such as creating a new file system, getting over perfectionism, or minimizing telephone time, you may fail to change any one habit. Apply to changing bad habits the "one thing at a time" approach.

Solution #3 — Devote at least 3 weeks to changing one habit.

Once you decide on a bad habit that you want to tackle—e. g., doing too many things at once, an inability to accept criticism, procrastination, perfectionism— spend at least twenty-one days changing that habit. As Young and Jones point out in *Sidetracked Home Executives*, the 21-day suggestion is based on research conducted by plastic surgeon Maxwell Maltz, author of *Psychocybernetics*. Maltz discovered that it took patients who had had a limb amputated twenty-one days to lose a ghost image of their missing limb.

Solution #4 — Seek out professional help.

Through referrals or recommendations, find a psychotherapist, psychologist, psychiatrist, or social worker with whom you have rapport who is trained to help someone to change bad habits.

Be realistic, however, that there are few "overnight cures." But whether it takes months, or years, to get at the root of the bad habits that sabotage you, you will be making permanent changes to serve you well. Another benefit: if you get to the bottom of your negative habits, you might avoid passing along those same bad habits to your children.

Solution#5 — Try behavior modification techniques.

This type of psychotherapy uses classic learning techniques to modify behavior including aversion therapy, biofeedback, and reinforcement.

Solution #6 — Join a self-help group.

There are self-help groups for practically every concern you might have including Messies Anonymous and Clutterers Anonymous. The web site http:///www.selfgrowth.com lists hundreds of self-help groups.

Solution #7 — Develop a new, positive habit to replace the current bad habit.

Replacing the undesirable habit, such as telephone interruptions, with a new, desirable habit, such as setting aside a specific time for placing, and receiving, calls will help overcome a bad habit.

Lateness

Lateness wastes everyone's time. If you're late, you are probably getting scores of people mad at you on a regular basis. If you have to deal with people who are chronically late, you are probably anywhere from angry to enraged by their behavior.

You can't control someone else's lateness, but you can help the situation by setting an excellent example. So start with yourself and commit to being on time, all the time.

Solution #1 — Determine if there is a pattern to your lateness.

Are you late only now and then or chronically? Perhaps you always arrive late at work or for business lunches across town. Perhaps you tend to be late for meetings you would rather not attend.

Consider your average workday. What time should you arrive at your office? At what time did you arrive this morning? Yesterday? Do you have a pattern of chronic lateness (whereby you were late more than twice in the last week)?

Solution #2 — Once you determine if there is a pattern, figure out what is causing it.

Now that you see the pattern to your lateness, consider any of the following possible causes:

Mechanical reasons:
Alarm clock did not go off or was set for the wrong time

Transportation problems:
Car broke down
Poor driving conditions
Train or subway delay

Behavioral reasons:
Underestimating how long each task takes (e.g. taking a shower)
Waiting for others

Possible psychological reasons:
Need to be yelled at or noticed
Anger at your boss
As a way of procrastinating to avoid something
Worry about home so reluctant to leave for work
Worry about work so you delay leaving for home

Consider whether the reason you were late today, or this week, is likely to reoccur. If the cause of the lateness was a one-time occurrence, such as a flat tire, you will obviously deal with your lateness differently than if it is due to a habit or routine that you may have to break, such as spending too much time over breakfast, which indicates a pattern of lateness that has to be corrected.

Solution #3 — Plan better.

If you have to be somewhere at a certain time, make appointments with yourself to serve as time checks along the way. For example, "At 6:30 I have to be in the shower. At 7:00, I have to be out the door."

Allow yourself extra time for last-minute emergencies, phone calls, or traffic jams.

You may also have to be more realistic about how long it takes, to get someone on the phone or to do something since lateness also applies to projects as well as appointments.

Solution #4 —— Affix a time that will get you somewhere on time that works for you.

If you have a chronic problem with lateness, tell yourself you have to get somewhere 15 minutes to half-an-hour earlier, and stick to that earlier arrival time, which, in your case, should get you there *on time*.

Solution #5 —— Put your answering machine or voice mail on as you are preparing to leave.

This will help minimize your temptation to take that one last phone call which will probably be the reason you are late. Even if you can get off the phone quickly, you may be ruder than you would otherwise have been if you were not trying to dash out the door.

Solution #6 —— To overcome lateness on projects, set realistic mini-deadlines.

You may have a tendency toward lateness on long-term projects because of poor planning or because your expectations about how much you can accomplish within a certain time frame is unrealistic. It will help if you create "mini-deadlines" to keep yourself (and your team) on track, rather than just one "big" deadline a year or more off in the distance.

It will also be helpful to you to develop and maintain a detailed **time log** of how long projects take, including any previous projects similar to this new one. In that way it may be easier to set more realistic time frames and deadlines for each current or future project so you are less likely to finish late.

Solution #7 —— If there are psychological reasons to your lateness, get help to overcome them.

If your lateness problem cannot be cured by planning better, or by simply avoiding getting into a long telephone conversation when you are supposed to be walking out the door, you may need outside help to overcome the psychological reasons behind your lateness. By being late, you are causing people to notice you, but in a negative way. Your lateness is making people angry at you, perhaps even yelling at you. You may need help understanding what is behind this self-destructive pattern.

In the next chapter, the fundamentals of getting organized are probed in greater depth.

5
Becoming Organized and More Effective

Organization is not an end in itself but a means to the end.
PETER F. DRUCKER (*The Practice of Management*)

Being organized means that you are able easily to locate one thing out of your many possessions. Your system should be able to handle information, envelopes, keys, stamps, the annual report, computer files, books, subscription magazines, newsletters, E-mails that you print out, last year's tax return, and your passport, for starters.

Remember that you are trying to find a system of organizing your activities and possessions (or tools) that is best for you. We all have thousands of activities or actions we must follow up on— from the publicity campaign for a new product or your best friend's birthday to writing a monthly progress report. What is at issue is: What organizational system will best utilize your time management strengths and help you to organize your activities or things?

The benefits of getting organized are quickly observed. Sam, 34, a disorganized professor, now is on top of things and able to handle more work and personal activities. Sam explains: "The more I manage to organize my time and work settings, the more I find I can get done." Sam accomplished this transformation by organizing his non-teaching work and leisure time into a fixed routine, "setting schedules and deadlines for projects."

There are those who appear to be "born" organizers, and those who seem to be forever misplacing and forgetting things. The economic costs of disorder are dramatically driven home if you cannot find a valuable or one particular crucial document, like a birth certificate. Not as obvious, but costly nonetheless, are the wasted minutes each day—adding up to hours each month— reluctantly spent on treasure hunts, routinely searching for needed materials. Have you ever been locked out because you forgot your keys, or searched for an hour for your eyeglasses, hidden under yesterday's newspaper? Did you forget someone's birthday? How about the meeting you missed because you mislaid the notice? How about those last minute dashes to the liquor or grocery store just before guests arrived? Have you ever had to say, "I would have called sooner but I couldn't find your phone number"?

In my workplace survey of 234 men and women, almost everyone answered "How much time do you spend *each day* searching for something?" by noting that they spend anywhere from 1 minute to 4 hours searching daily, with the majority searching from 1 to 20 minutes. When I added up the total time that all these men and women are spending searching daily for something, it equals nearly 118.5 hours, or almost 3 full work weeks, that is collectively wasted in these searches.

Top five reasons for the search (in descending order)
1. Trying to find *a telephone number on a piece of paper or an address*. (27%)
2. Trying to *find current work-in-progress*. (24%)
3. Searching for *a contact person for follow-up* or *information about an upcoming meeting*. (15%)
4. Trying *to locate a file folder*. (14%)
5. Trying *to locate a file on a computer disk or hard drive*. (10%)*

*These percentages do not add up to 100% because there are additional #1 reasons chosen by the remaining respondents for the search that are not included in these five reasons. Those reasons include: searching for a book, magazine or newspaper clipping; incoming mail; going through a suitcase that was not yet unpacked; and something misfiled.

Thirteen men and women listed their #1 reason for their daily search was their car keys, house keys, or eyeglasses.

These numbers are tangible evidence of just some of the actual time that is being wasted in offices throughout the world because of disorganization. Beyond the time that is wasted in these searches is the anxiety, tension, frustration, and probably more than a few missed deadlines or miffed managers or clients.

Fortunately, there is hope and concrete help for creating more order and organization in your work and life. In this chapter you will find a discussion of basic organizational principles, as well as several suggested systems; but one of your own creation is, if it works, perhaps even better. Follow this basic principle: Never make the system your focus; the system is supposed to make things easier. If you spend too much time creating, and maintaining, your "system," its purpose is lost.

Extreme disorder and extreme order will both prove to be wasteful of time.

You want to learn how to better organize your thoughts and actions as well as your possessions. Those three elements usually go together. There are exceptions, such as when you are working on a project and need to put everything aside, including filing, till you reach a certain point in your work, but often a continually cluttered desk reflects a cluttered mind. Throughout this chapter remember that your goal is becoming organized in what you do and how you do it but in the service of your overall goal of becoming more productive.

GETTING ORGANIZED

Take a few moments to reflect on the time management strengths observed in the offices of effective and organized individuals:

1. Promptness.

2. Scheduling appointments based on accurate estimates of how long tasks (procedures) will take.

3. Notes and reminders written down in one book, or in an electronic organizer, not on pieces of paper that create unmanageable piles.

4. Notes, and appointments, written in pencil to facilitate corrections.

5. Minimal personal phone or in-person interruptions. If such interruptions do occur, they are handled quickly (and in private).

6. Showing interest in work-related relations by: a) listening; b) making interesting small talk; c) keeping personal problems to oneself; and d) giving explanations in clear but not condescending language.

7. Maintaining a daily "things to do" list.

8. Deciding on, and following through on, short term priorities and long term plans.

9. Dealing with coworkers, clients, and employees in a formal but pleasant manner.

10. Scheduling personal time off for vacations.

11. Replacing files or tools in their proper place after each use.

Being Organized is a Trait You Can Learn

Disorganization frustrates the best attempts to effectively use your time. There are some who gain enormous pleasure from cleaning out their closets and ordering their activities or possessions. However, it's a lot easier to entrust organizing your possessions to someone else than it is to revamp *how* you go about your business or leisure activities.

Have a master plan to your activities. If you are in control of what you do, you will be more effective. Being organized is a tool to increasing your effectiveness.

How do you organize your business or personal affairs? Do you feel "in control" of your everyday activities, or as if you are bouncing off this crisis or that demand? What are your time management strengths? Does your present work or home routine take full advantage of those strengths? Perhaps you work best in long stretches, but you currently interrupt yourself for a one hour lunch at the same time each day since that's what's expected of you, or so you think. Could you take a later lunch, or order lunch in and take a break later on in the day, to aid your work productivity?

You may find that you need to try, revise, and disregard certain schedules and procedures in order to become more organized and effective in what you do. As the demands on your time have changed—and as your goals and values have altered—you need to ask yourself whether your time budget reflects those changes.

Organizing your possessions makes possible more effective use of your time at work and home. Your goal is not to look organized, but to *be* organized. We have all heard of that rare individual who, faced with an elbow high stack of papers, can miraculously pull out of it the one scrap of paper that he needs. To everyone but him, that stack is a mess; but that mess is his order.

If you are unlike that fictional character—and most of us are—becoming organized will take some effort. "Right places" for everything have to be created, so you'll know where to look for things later. Apply an organizing principle to your activities, whether that system is chronological, thematic, general to specific, or specific to general. Impose order on your work, or possessions, if they lack a "natural" order. Example: you have a conference to plan and you need an organizing principle for how you go about planning it. Create a principle by deciding tasks to do in the order of their importance, or in chronological order (e.g. picking a date, finding a location, lining up speakers, creating a brochure.)

Here are four simple organizational guidelines:

1. Eliminate Clutter.
2. Everything in its place.
3. Plan what you have to do and make sure you do it.
4. Group and do similar tasks together.

Distinguishing Daily Priorities from Busywork

If at day's end you cannot point to one productive activity, you are allowing busywork, related to work or personal affairs, to interfere with accomplishing your short term priorities "one day at a time" and your long term goals.

Even if your office job has someone else assigning specific work to you, you may be taking longer than you would like to accomplish those projects. Or you may be failing to accomplish job-related goals for your own advancement. For example, if you need to rewrite your resume, or acquire new skills to add to your areas of expertise, the burden will probably be on you to find the time to do it during your non-work hours.

Busywork is another term for low-priority tasks. Having a third cup of coffee as you read the third city newspaper is probably busywork, unless you work for a newspaper clipping service. You may wish you "did more"at work, but because of poor planning, procrastination, or spending too long on low-priority calls to you (rather than placing those high priority calls that can make the difference in your job or business), you are frustrated by your low productivity.

Two of the biggest inhibitors to being organized and effective are **paperwork** and **telephone calls**. Paperwork can generate hours of busywork. A distinction has to be made between high-priority paperwork, discussed in the next chapter under *"Correspondence and Paperwork,"* and doing the paper shuttle, whereby papers (junk mail, low priority pieces of paper, material to be filed or discarded) are moved around, or piled up in a disorganized fashion, consuming time and space.

You've probably already heard lots of advice on paperwork, like "Handle a piece of paper only once" or " Dot a piece of paper each time you handle it until it has the measles and you do something with it." Doing the paper shuffle, described more extensively in the next chapter, can be an enormous time drain. Minimize your chances of falling into the paper busywork trap by eliminating distracting papers as much as possible. File it. Answer it. Throw it out. Put it with other papers of a similar nature and take care of them all at once.

Telephone calls may also consume hours of valuable time. If you personally take each and every call as it comes in, interrupting whatever you are doing at that moment, how do you expect to be organized? Try scheduling a telephone hour for placing calls—you have more control over when you place calls than when they come in—and budget that hour into your daily schedule.

You might also try instituting a period during the morning and the afternoon at the office when you prefer to receive incoming calls. Write lists, for yourself or your secretary, if you have one, of telephone interruptions that are permissible at times other than your designated "incoming-call hours." (The more strictly you adhere to your "no calls now" policy, the more valuable this way of organizing your day will become.) If you use a cell phone, you might consider getting voice mail on your phone so that callers may leave a message for you. In that way, you will be more likely to avoid automatically answering the phone if there is a safety concern, such as when you are driving, or if you are in the midst of a meeting, project, or conversation.

At home, consider that, except for emergencies, telephone calls should not be allowed to interfere with your dinnertime (often the only time some families have to interact with each other). Say to callers: "We're having dinner now. Can I call you back later?" If you're consistent, your friends, relatives, and even business associates will learn to respect your personal time budget.

Sharpening Decision-Making Skills

Becoming more organized and effective means sharpening your decision-making skills. By making clear decisions you will eliminate clutter because you will decide what to do with each and every piece of paper that comes into your office or passes across your desk.

Postponing decisions about what to do with paper, catalogues, reports, or even phone messages on slips of paper will lead to clutter and the companion to clutter, disorganization.

To sharpen your decision-making, develop well-conceived rules upon which you base decisions. In that way, you will avoid the need to ponder every little situation. Ask yourself these questions any time a decision has to be made:

How important is this to do?
What are the consequences of doing it? not doing it?
Why do it now? the consequences of doing it later?
How does this new idea (situation, request, etc.) fit in with what's important to me now? for the rest of my life?

By applying the rule of "What is :ny number one priority right now?" you will sharpen your decision-making skills. You will also sharpen your decision-making, and save time, if you focus on learning, not assessing blame. If a new idea or approach is suggested to you, ask yourself: Is it faster (or better)? Is it slower (or less effective)? What makes the difference? Reducing or eliminating the obstacles to effective time management discussed in Chapters 3 and 4, as well as becoming more organized, will also facilitate your decision-making skills.

ORGANIZING TOOLS AND TECHNIQUES

"To Do" Lists

Mental order is even more important than cataloging your possessions. One of the most effective tools in time management is knowing what you have to do. Maintain a "things to do" list, and write it down. Make sure it's readily accessible to you.

There are several approaches to creating "things to do" list. Such a list makes it more likely that you will act on important matters. Time management expert Merrill E. Douglass offers this advice about effective "to do" lists:

Frankly, the To-Do lists that are kept by most people provide only marginal benefits. The reason is that most To Do lists are a random collection of activities which have very little, if anything, to do with the purpose for which people work. Furthermore, most people have such a poor grasp of their objectives and priorities that a To Do list can hardly be an improvement. Thirdly, almost no one gives real thought to how long things take. As a consequence, most To Do lists contain far more than could be done in any given day. An excellent To Do list asks a very critical question: "How long is it going to take me to do it?"

Here are some alternative ways for creating effective "to do" lists for your work and personal goals:

(A) Divide your list to reflect how you arrange your day, such as:

1. Before Work
2. During Work
3. After Work

Within each section, fill in the appropriate activities.

(B) Follow a simpler chronological system, listing the key activities you want to accomplish that day, starting with number one. As you finish an activity, check or cross it off, and go on to the next thing you have to do. A sample of this approach follows:

1. Call airline or go on Internet to purchase tickets.
2. Write memo for meeting.
3. Duplicate memo for distribution.

(C) Write items down in order of descending importance, putting the major daily goal as number one (and not going on to number two until number one is done). Obviously, you will have to break down large tasks— writing a term paper, preparing a speech—into smaller steps, or you may take weeks to get to number two. Here's a sample of that approach:

1. Writing memo for meeting.
2. Duplicate memo for distribution.
3. Call airline or go on Internet to order tickets.

(D) Use the verb-noun principle discussed in the 4th principle of creative time management, "Keep your focus," on pages 11-12. That system is especially useful if you have to complete a major project but you find yourself procrastinating or getting distracted by activities of lesser importance.

Create a "things to do" list and check off each item as you complete it. Include all personal and professional tasks. Decide which organizing principle you will follow, and start by attacking whatever "to-do" item is first on your list.

The idea is not to become a list maker, spending more time in creating lists than in completing your priority tasks. List making is merely a way to organize your obligations—and a way to learn to do thoroughly one thing at a time.

Practically everyone I interviewed who finds list making useful preferred writing a "to-do" list for the following day right before going to bed; some said it actually helped them to sleep better. John, 31, a self-employed glass designer, says: "Between midnight and one, I make a list of items to do the next day. Some are important to do that day and I do those first. Others may be done another day, but I write them down when I think of them."

Creating a Personal Planning Calendar

The importance of a personal planning calendar is emphasized when, because of failure to maintain one, appointments are missed, deadlines ignored, or details of upcoming events are confused. Just in the past week, for example, Gloria showed up a week early for a party, Jim and Claudia forgot their daughter's wedding anniversary, and George had to cancel two meetings because he had failed to note that he would be away on jury duty. Alas, creating a personal planning calendar will not prevent others, who lack one, from disappointing you. However, it ensures that you will be more organized and efficient.

Bonnie, 28, vice-president of a bank, credits her organizational savvy to her personal planning calendar. Without fail, she records all work and personal commitments on that calendar. "It helps me to sleep at night," Bonnie explains. In one place she notes birthdays to remember, upcoming meetings, seminars she has to attend, and vacation days.

Your planning calendar can be a wall calendar, a daily appointment book—whether on traditional paper or an electronic version—but the consensus is that all the information should be kept in one place.

Depending on the work or personal demands on your schedule, you might need to have a calendar of the entire year at your fingertips if, let's say, you want to see the date in April you're scheduled to speak in Denver and the date in June you're scheduled to do a seminar in St. Paul.

Try to get into the habit of recording events as well as preparation time. For instance, you have to give a talk on Saturday, May twenty-first, and, of course, that is noted in your daily appointment book or on your wall chart. Have you also noted what hours or days you will be devoting to the preparation of that talk, including research time and practice sessions?

Remember: apply the same organization rules to your activities as you will apply to organizing your possessions. Eliminate clutter, unnecessary time wasters and interruptions, poor planning, and disorder.

Your planning calendar should provide you with an overview of specific commitments for the days, weeks, and months ahead. If possible, use pencil, so corrections are facilitated. Make sure you note personal plans or you might forget to follow up on them. Consider entering "free day" on your planning calendar, or you may never find the time for one.

The Everything Notebook

A variation on the personal planning calendar is the personal notebook. Like the calendar, all notes, incoming and outgoing phone calls, new addresses and phone numbers, ideas, and random thoughts are jotted down in one place as they occur. The notebook, such as a small spiral, looseleaf, or bound notebook, if possible, is carried with you at all times—in your pants or jacket pocket, pocketbook or attaché case. The advantage of using one notebook, what travel writer Theodore Fischer calls his "Everything Notebook," is that you avoid the disorganized mess of lots of little slips of papers that may be lost, misplaced, or in need of being transferred to another source. (You may still decide to transfer some of your notes and memos, but you always have your master chronological source to refer to.) The Everything Notebook is labeled with the current year. If more than one notebook is used during the year, each volume is numbered consecutively. As Fischer explains:

> This way I have only one source to go to; only one thing to grab when the phone rings. Every bit of business goes into the notebook. Each one lasts about two to three months. I'd feel undressed if I didn't have this book with me. One other thing about the notebooks: each time one is full, I have to decide which names, numbers, and addresses to copy into the new book. This provides a valuable opportunity for taking personal, social, and professional stock because you have to determine which names are still important, which are no longer important, which may be potentially important.

If you prefer an electronic or computer version of the Everything Notebook concept, there are numerous products available to you, from hand-held computers or devices that will synchronize with your desktop computer, like the PalmPilot,™ as well as writing tablets that are linked to your computer.

Be open to these innovative systems as well as the ever-changing new technology becoming available at a faster and faster pace. Go to electronic trade shows, stop in and talk with sales representatives, or ask a colleague or friend who uses a system if he or she will take some time to demonstrate it for you, and see if these electronic notebooks could help you to keep your thoughts and data organized.

File Systems

The main types of materials that will fill your home or office files are:

1. Originals of incoming correspondence and/or interoffice memos.
2. Copies of outgoing correspondence.
3. Important papers, documents, or records for permanent safekeeping.
4. Reference or research materials.
5. Warranties (and any related receipts), and instruction booklets.
6. Announcements about upcoming meetings or events.

How many files you need will depend upon the kind of job you do, and how much information or material you want or need to have available. (The term *file* as it is used throughout this section refers to the conventional beige manila letter-size file folder. File could also mean oversized envelopes, floppy disks, or magnetic diskettes, or index cards.)

Keep active and inactive items separated, so that you can find day-to-day and priority materials quickly.

Once you decide which files you need ready access to, the major battle against disorganization of papers and research materials is won. Once you create a system, based upon inactive and active categories, it will be much easier to find things.

Within your active files, there are several basic organizing principles to follow for sorting your papers and labeling the files:

1. **Chronologically (by date).** Going from current backwards, or

vice versa.

2. **Numerically.** Give each item listed or displayed in a master file a number and give each file folder a matching number to that item.

3. **Alphabetically.** If files are for individuals, file by last name, followed by first name. For topics or titles, file by the first letter of the first key word (not by an "a" or a "the.") For titles, you might also consider alphabetizing by the author's last, then first name.

4. **By subject or topic category.**

5. **By immediacy or importance (the priority approach).** Ordering based on the immediacy of response required or the urgency of the material in the file.

6. **By color.** Color coding with a master file identifying what each color signifies.

You can arrange research material alphabetically or by subjects (broad or narrow). You can put important documents in a file broadly labeled " important records" or put each record or document in a separate file; those files can then be organized by category, alphabetically, chronologically, by subject, or by color.

The overruling primary concern for an excellent filing system: in a month, a year, or ten years, will I be able to quickly find this material, or file, again or will I be able to easily explain to someone else where this file is located? If your answer is "yes," you are probably using an effective system.

There is one type of written material that must be filed, and it might be helpful to keep that file separate from the day-to-day originals and copies of memos that you also need to file. These crucial documents are the CY ("Cover Yourself") materials. You might also wish to cross-file these key materials: by category or in the regular file and in the CY special file. That way, if a problem does arise an hour, a day, a week, or even a year or two from now, you can show, through your careful records (the CY file), that you were not at fault, because you had touched second base, notified the appropriate governmental agency within the filing deadline, or made the necessary payment.

Try devising a new or improved filing system:

Step 1: Divide a blank sheet of paper into two columns labeled "Active" and "Inactive."

Step 2: Make a list of all the types of materials that you need to file, such as incoming correspondence, canceled checks, and documents, placing each category under the "Active" or "Inactive" heading (duplicating entries under both headings, if appropriate.)

Step 3: Select one type of material to be filed—e.g., incoming correspondence— and decide what filing system you will use.

Step 4: On a blank sheet of paper, work out on paper how you plan to file that one category, noting the organizing principle that you will follow, the system to be used, who will have ready access to these files, and a way in which active material can be rendered inactive.

Step 5: On separate sheets, repeat this paper planning process for your remaining categories.

Step 6: In order of importance, begin to implement your filing systems, purchasing any necessary supplies. Continue until your files are created.

Step 7: Maintain your planning notes, a help to you if at any point you forget any of the details behind your system.

Another filing system that some effective managers find useful is called a "tickler file." The system works like this: A file folder is made for each day of the month so that there are thirty or thirty-one file folders numbered one through thirty-one. There are also twelve files, one for each month. Any follow-up items are placed in the appropriate "to do" month file; as the month becomes current, pieces of paper are moved to the specific date (file) on which the action is to be carried out.

The tickler file requires some time to set up. For it to be effective, you have to maintain, and use it, as consistently as your daily planning calendar. For example, you might buy enough birthday and anniversary cards for the entire year. Address the envelopes and place the blank cards in the appropriate month when you will need one. When the month arrives, you move the card to the file for the date on which you should inscribe and mail that card. If you have season tickets to sports events, concerts, and so forth, you could file the appropriate tickets with the correct month, moving the tickets to the appropriate date as that month becomes current.

If you use a computer or word processor, there is software available that has calendars and reminders that perform a function that is similar to the "tickler" file. Two such software organizing programs are Day-Timer® Organizer 2000 and and OneStep Connect Personal Organizer. But you may still, however, want some kind of filing system for placing the actual correspondence, memos, cards, or tickets that you are following up on.

Types of possible filing systems include: filing cabinets of all sizes and shapes; document folders; magnetic diskettes (for use with computers/word processors); envelopes; boxes (cardboard, metal, or plastic); containers (decorative or plain); looseleaf notebooks; bound or spiral notebooks; garbage can; or bulletin board. You may find that the system that works best for you is just one of these filing options, or a more eclectic system that combines looseleaf notebooks for certain material, like weekly newsletters arranged chronologically, file cabinets with files arranged chronologically or alphabetically, and boxes for keeping all the material (piles) related to a current project before filing in file cabinets once the project is completed.Using a definite filing *system* to keep your work and materials organized frees up your memory for more important storage—the kind that can't be handled by filing.

The 30-Day File Diet

Quick access to the right information is vital today especially as the information explosion has caused a proliferation of data to be stored, and retrieved.

Streamlined and tightly organized files are one way to make sure you stay on top of the growing information, instead of being buried by it. Thinner files will usually help you get your job done better and more efficiently. Since additional file cabinets cost money and occupy costly office space, thin files will also help a company to keep down its costs.

Step # 1 Pick a target date.

By picking a definite date to thin out your files, you will overcome the biggest obstacle to thin files--procrastination. Mini case history: a midwestern data processing technology supplier picked the company's move to new offices as the target date for its first company-wide file purging program. The 350 headquarters employees were instructed to thin out their files since fewer files meant a less expensive move as well as fewer file cabinets-and more space-in the new offices. To boost employee motivation, the company came up with a charity incentive: for every pound of purged paper, the company would donate a pound of food to a local hunger group to feed the needy.

Just how much paper was purged? Thirteen tons of paper were purged or, to put that into more concrete terms, the paper that was thrown out enabled the company to discard 80 two-drawer lateral files. The campaign was so successful that the company made it an annual event.

Step #2 Be prepared for your file purging.

Have on hand a large empty garbage can and a recycling bin to aid your thinning efforts. Have strong string available if you need to tie up discarded catalogs or magazines for recycling or disposal. If practical in your office setting, if music makes the task more pleasant, have on hand a radio, cassette or CD player.

Step #3 Pick the best time to do your purging.

Whether you work in an outside office, or a home-based one, find a time to prune and purge your files that is convenient for you. If it is hard to find time during the workday, you may want to come in earlier, or over a weekend or holiday. Those with a home-based business may prefer to file in the evening, very early in the morning, before the workday begins, or over the weekend.

Having someone help you sort through your files is another tactic to keep you on track. Budget time for file management.

Step #4 Have clear reasons for keeping or purging material.

Grab a file. It could be the first file in your drawer or a specific category that is especially thick. Now ask yourself the following questions that Cecilia McKenzie, records expert and compliance analyst at Champion International, suggests you consider:
1. Is the information of value?
2. Will it add something new to what I have?
3. Can I obtain it elsewhere?
4. Is it significant for the company's purpose?

Answers to those questions will help you decide if you should hold on to a piece of paper, pass it along to someone else, or throw it in the garbage can or recycling bin.

Step # 5 Thin out files according to your particular filing system.

Use this thinning-out task to clarify your filing system or, if you lack one, to implement one. The better your overall file system, the easier it will be to thin out each file. It could be a system that is alphabetical, chronological, geographic, by subject, by color, by urgency, or an eclectic combination of all six. Example: Require that each file contains a key piece of paper, and that the essential item is the *first* piece of paper in the file.

Whatever your system, having one will facilitate thinner files.

Colored hanging files can add to effectiveness. If one drawer only contains files that are paid and they're all in orange file folders, and all the ones with a debit have green file folders in another place, it reduces the likelihood that someone will accidentally put a debit account in a paid account. When you group things that relate to each other in the same place, it means you use less space.

Step #6 Discard multiple copies or outdated materials.

Shred, throw out, or recycle outdated reports or other obsolete materials that are unnecessary for reference.

Step # 7 Know what you should keep, and for how long.

Your company (or your accountant) may have specific guidelines for a retention and purge schedule for certain kinds of documents. Check with the company's records personnel, lawyer, or accountant.

Step #8 Reward yourself for thinner files.

Now that you've thinned out your files, indulge yourself with something you never find time for but like to do.

Step #9 Establish and maintain a regular sift-and-purge schedule.

Keep on top of your files by instituting a regular pruning schedule, such as once a week or monthly. Consider writing the purge date on each file, or noting it through color coding techniques. See filing as a necessary part of being organized, and in control, of your files. A well-maintained file system will enable you to find what you need quickly, and efficiently, thereby contributing to your goal of creative time management.

Organizing Your Office

Out of 113 who completed a survey on the office that I tabulated for my book on the office (*Making Your Office Work For You*), only five noted that if they could change their office they would redecorate it. For everyone else (89 out of 113), an organizational or physical change, such as a better-organized office, more space or privacy, less noise, or improved lighting, were the key concerns.

My four year original research into the office discovered three principles for organizing an office:

1. productivity
2. status or image
3. a combination of #1 and #2

If your work is your calling card, and you rarely have visitors to your office, such as most writers, artists, salespersons who are on the road most of the time, productivity will probably be the key element to how your office is organized.

Offices organized around status or image use the office as a way of indicating a company's status as well as the position someone occupies in a company. The cues to that status are usually the size of the office, its location on a floor in terms of proximity to one's superiors, or on another floor, whether or not there is a window, if it is the coveted corner office, and the quality of the furniture, artifacts, and wall hangings. But even if you work alone in an outside office, or work from home, having an attractive and efficient office may boost your self-esteem and self-worth thereby boosting your productivity and probably your net worth as well.

Look at the office space you have. Are you in an open office setting without any privacy? Is this having a negative impact on your productivity? Is there anyway to achieve privacy, such as turning your chair and back away from others working nearby?

If you have an office with a door, could you rearrange your furniture to maximize your productivity? Is your office organized for peak efficiency? If you find there are too many drop-in visitors sitting and talking, have you considered removing the extra chair in your office, or replacing a thick upholstered chair with an uncomfortable metal or wooden one?

Health Considerations

Here are some of the health-related issues to consider when you organize your office:

- air quality.
- noise levels.
- eyestrain caused by improper lighting or improperly-used equipment, such as photocopy machines.
- backaches due to poorly-designed workstations, desks, chairs, or too much sedentary work.
- back or leg injuries due to poorly-organized offices such as poorly-positioned file cabinets, open drawers, boxes that block aisles, improperly lifting too-heavy objects or cartons.
- minimizing conditions that contribute to stress and fatigue.

Organizing Your Desk

Your primary goal is to avoid unmanageable and disorderly piles of unrelated supplies and materials in or on your desk. You want everything readily accessible, and in a place of its own. Keep extras of all your supplies, in ample quantity, in a supply closet or another storage area. If possible, have a wastebasket within reach.

Organizing the top of your desk is quite an individual matter but if you have a problem concentrating at your desk, try experimenting with adding or removing items—e.g.. family portraits, pencil holders, paper weights, stapler, tape dispenser, or calendars—to see if your work habits improve.

If possible, you should avoid keeping anything other than your current work on top of your desk— too many files or projects can provoke the "doing too much at once" syndrome. Jessica, 60, a middle management executive, has such a cluttered desk (and office) that she has to find a vacant office at her company to meet with clients. "I never get around to cleaning my desk because I always feel I should be doing real work," Jessica explains. Keeping your desk organized is part of every job. Fortunately, once the initial organizational system is implemented, it takes just minutes each day to maintain it.

Here are three useful tips for organizing your office:
1. **Schedule time for organizing, writing it down on your calendar.**
2. **Have a regular "file purging" day for computer and paper files.**
3. **If you need help reorganizing your office, consider hiring a professional to help you set up your initial systems even if you and your staff regularly maintain it.** Contact the National Association of Professional Organizers (NAPO), for referrals. NAPO is at 1033 La Posada Drive, Suite 220, Austin, Texas 78752-3880. For information and referrals: 512-206-0151 or visit their web site: www.napo.net.

Books, Magazines, and Other Reading Materials

Books, magazines, newspapers, journals, pamphlets, and other reading materials pile up quickly, and can become a major obstacle to an organized office or home. One couple has let the problem get so out of hand that whenever they move, their multiple cartons of unsorted reading materials move with them. The thought of going through those boxes, organizing useful materials and discarding the rest, is more awesome than spending the time and money to continually transport those weighty boxes.

Before it gets out of hand, you will find it a great time saver to evolve an orderly system for the accumulation, and disposal, of reading materials. Have a clear notion of whether you will sort or discard on a daily, weekly, monthly, or yearly basis.

There are a variety of temporary storage systems for reading materials— baskets for the floor or your desk, lucite holders, vertical cardboard units, elaborate 48 or 96 compartment literature organizers, etc.—that you can use for sorting and storing reading materials. You might also consider the altruistic and tax benefits of donating reading materials, that you might otherwise throw out, to college or local libraries, or schools.

Bookcases should fit the space available to you and be of the correct size for what you have to shelve. If you don't want to take the time to measure the height needed for each shelf, get adjustable shelves.

Arranging books by category, author, or another system geared to your needs will, in the long run, save you time, but initially you will have to devote some time to completing that task (depending on how many books you have). Remove the books from the shelves and rearrange one section at a time, working in a systematic way from top to bottom or left to right.

Just as you made a list of incoming magazines and other reading materials, now make a list of the categories of books that you have. If you find that your collection is basically just one or two types of books—let's say reference books such as the dictionary, a grammar book, and works of fiction—you might decide that it is more efficient for you to organize within the fiction section, by author or by title, with a second section for reference books, by title.

One way you can save lots of space and time today is by having at least one CD-ROM version of major reference works, usually updated annually. On just one disk, you could have an entire encyclopedia as well as a dictionary. (Recycle or dispose of outdated disks as CD-ROM disks can pile up and create clutter.)

In the Home Office

Two hundred years ago, as a result of the industrial revolution, work and living space separated. Working from home, however, has become increasingly popular in the last few decades. Because of the computer, and the widespread availability of overnight mail, Internet access, E-mail, and fax machines, as well as the time and expense saved by avoiding a daily commute to work, more office workers than ever before are working at home, some or all of the time.

If you work at home, you have more pressure to become, and stay, organized than most other workers since visitors to your home may also have access to your office.

Even if your home office is a completely separate room, with a door that could close it off to wandering eyes or visitors, the more organized and less cluttered you are, the less likely that anyone waltzing through your office, including children, a spouse, or visitors, could ruin or obscure your work.

Obviously your organizational problems will be somewhat different if your home office is a separate room in a spacious home, or in the corner of the living room in a two-bedroom apartment that you share with a spouse and two children. Certain considerations are universal, however: what are the essential supplies and equipment that have to be nearby and what can be stored elsewhere—in closets, other rooms, even other locations?

Here are additional tips to optimize home office productivity:

1. Make the first thing you do when you get into your home office the most important project of the day.
2. Avoid doing household chores or errands during the workday.
3. Keep a regular schedule. Make sure the phones are covered when you are out of the office.
4. Get a separate phone line for your home office and train your children or spouse not to answer it; use voice mail, an answering machine, or an answering service instead.
5. Take time for lunch and efficiency breaks every few hours if you work in long stretches.
6. To offset the potential emotional and professional isolation that working from home could cause, become active in at least one professional association.
7. Try to attend monthly breakfast, luncheon, or after work get togethers or meetings for social reasons and to keep up in your field.
8. Almost all home-based workers, if you have very young children at home, will need additional childcare help if you are to work more than just during your child's naptime or sleeptime hours.
9. Tell your friends not to call you during business hours.
10. Be flexible. If working from home used to be okay but now you need employees or more space, consider an outside office.

The next chapter provides additional suggestions for improved work productivity, whether you work in an outside or home office.

6
Improving Your Time at Work

More men are killed by overwork than the importance of the world justifies.
———RUDYARD KIPLING (*The Phantom Rickshaw*)

In some ways, the structure of the traditional work environment aids time management: although there may be autonomy within each task, employers set rules or guidelines about when to arrive, when to leave, what days to take as holidays, and, often, what to wear. However, procedures for evaluating performance and determining a raise are not always as clearly defined.

Within this framework, then, you are to a large extent on your own. You may know that you have to go to a meeting on Wednesday, but no one tells you how to get the most out of it. So don't let the external structure of your job misguide you that if you just show up each day, follow the rules, and do what's asked, you'll be making the best use of your time (and guaranteeing success.) The hard part of your workday is completely up to you. Although following company policy may seem commendable, that's the very least that's expected. Those rules go along with the job: observe them or quit. But what you do with the work that you're given is what will help you stand out from everyone else, sending you up the ladder, or back to the mailroom.

When it comes to work (or school), ask yourself this question: Is my performance judged on the quality of what I do, the volume of work I generate or complete, or whether or not I meet deadlines? Perhaps it's all three or, perhaps, it changes from day to day, month to month, or project to project. But this is a question that you should be continually asking yourself.

To improve your time at work or in business first make sure you know exactly what is expected of you.

First do what's expected; the extras are the gravy. If you're hired for your contract negotiating skills, but you're wheeling and dealing to try to bring in new clients instead, the person who hired you might not be as pleased as you thought she would be.

UNDERSTANDING YOUR WORK ENVIRONMENT

Laura punches in each morning exactly at nine and goes to the three-walled, metal cubicle in a high-rise office building where she will spend the next eight hours, minus one hour for lunch.

On the surface she is an excellent, reliable worker. She does not need to take work home; she seems to accomplish it all within her workday. She takes two weeks off each year for her paid vacation, all the sick days and personal leave that she is allowed, and she seems always to be busy. Underneath the "perfect employee" facade, however, are these realities: at least two hours are spent on the phone with up to 25 personal calls daily; Laura is not given enough to do, so she reads novels and magazines carefully concealed from her boss, whose office is many cubicles away; She spends a lot of time in traveling to and from the bathroom, chatting all the way.

Those who work hard and are surprised by Laura's lackadaisical attitude might believe that management soon "found out" Laura's ways. They didn't! Laura learned how to get management's expectations lowered to her own standard. When Laura left to take a better offer (and more money), she was sent on her way with roses and glowing letters of recommendation.

There are many who would not want to trade places with Laura even if they could. Job satisfaction means accomplishing a job that you value, not just getting paid for sitting at a desk all day, doing as little as you can get away with.

Some office workers say: "I can only get things done before everyone else gets here" (or after everyone else leaves). The result: they work seven to five or nine to seven, but not all that time is spent well. Their work-related time is longer, yet not necessarily more productive.

Take a hard, critical look at your workday. Write down the demands on you. Keep a time log to see where your time goes.

Managing your time better at work may mean redesigning your work space so you have better working conditions. It might mean asking your boss if you can get a door for your cubicle, because socializing with employees has so gotten out of hand that you find you have less and less uninterrupted time.

You might even consider talking to your employer about the possibility of flexible working hours, also known as flextime—an alternative to traditional fixed work schedules that gives you more flexibility to choose the times of your arrival and departure, and sometimes even the days that you work.

It is up to you, as much as possible within managerial or economic restraints, to make your work environment as efficient, pleasant, and functional as possible. Apply the conceptual and practical organizing principles that you learned in the previous chapter: everything in its place; eliminate clutter; and have readily available the tools and supplies you frequently need.

Becoming More Efficient

Correspondence and Paperwork

Practically all office jobs require writing, and answering, letters; even if you delegate the actual writing of your correspondence to a secretary or an assistant, an incoming letter has to be read and a decision made about whether it should be answered, and what form that answer will take.

Correspondence can become so time-consuming that the real work never gets done. It can also be so integral to your work that without it, there will be no real work. It's best to use correspondence as a warm-up up for the more demanding, or creative, parts of your job.

Michael Korda, editor chief at Simon & Schuster publishing company as well as the best selling author of *Power!* and *Success!*, finds that doing his own mail in the morning is a way he uses his "energy potential," as he puts it in *Success!*:

> ...then I decided that it was important to begin the day by accomplishing something, however trivial. I would spend the first hour of the morning answering mail. I would take no telephone calls, see nobody. I treated the mail as a separate, important but finite block of work. When I had read it, answered it, taken the necessary action where action was called for and gotten rid of it all, I had a cup of coffee, took a walk around the office to see what was happening, then went back to answer telephone calls on a priority basis. It was not very long before I began to look forward to my first hour—it gave me a sense of accomplishment and purpose.

Korda essentially found a way to turn the tedious task of answering correspondence into something motivational.

If you have a tendency to procrastinate about correspondence, address the envelopes and keep them in front of you. It may help to motivate you to write the letters that have to go inside those envelopes.

Dictating correspondence into a tape recorder is useful if you are experiencing "writer's block." However, traditional dictating letters may waste time since you or your assistant will have to first transcribe the tape and then write the letter.Consider voice recognition software which enable you to speak into a computer, even a hand-held one; the computer recognizes your voice and creates a written version for you or your assistant to edit.

You may also save time by having several "types" of letters for you, or your secretary, to adapt according to specific circumstances, such as business letters that say "Thank you," "Sorry, no jobs are currently available," "May I have the following information. . ." and so forth. These samples differ from a form letter in that they are adapted to a specific person and situation. They are not photocopied nor do they resemble a letter done *en masse* on a word processor.

If you do use a computer, and the body of the letter, make your modified "form" letter as short as possible. One-to-two page single-spaced letters are often a "tip off" that they have been done on a computer.

Computer templates are available for correspondence; these samples of letters, both for wording and for style, are a starting point for correspondence that you or your assistant could customize.

Business correspondence, like phone calls, should be responded to as promptly as possible.

To save time, if appropriate, consider sending an E-mail or a brief memo, rather than a more time-consuming formal business letter.

Some time management experts, such as Alan Lakein, advise: "Handle each piece of paper only once." That advice, like all time management advice, has to be tailored to your own needs. If you tend to procrastinate, are unable to discriminate between priority and low-payoff correspondence, or if out-of-sight is out-of-mind, this more conventional time management approach of handling a piece of paper just once may serve you better than filing paper according to a specific category, to be retrieved, and dealt with, at a later date.

As was noted in the previous chapter on becoming organized, the key is to set up a filing system that works for you. It doesn't matter if it's alphabetic, chronological, thematic, by color, coding by number, or whatever. All that counts is that you can find things in a fast and reliable manner.

How you handle copies of materials can be crucial; over time, paper has a way of piling up and becoming unmanageable. A lawyer I know makes two copies of each memo or letter; one is filed by subject; the other is filed chronologically. This way he has two ways of relocating it at some point in the future.

Do you regularly copy all important memos? Do you make notes about telephone conversations and put them into your files? Keeping track of what you accomplish each day is a way of gaining control of your time. But do not make the written record, or copies of that record, as important as the work itself.

Technology and Tools for Effective Time Management

According to my work survey, a majority (52%) of the men and women who answered a question about what technological advance has been their best time-saver over the last decade checked off personal computer (PC). A very distant second was the fax machine (16%) followed by E-mail (12%), which is actually tied to the computer. [Number 4 was the microwave (less than 1%) and number 5 was the cell phone (less than 1%).]

Technology and equipment, whether it is a computer, a photocopying or a fax machine, can save, as well as waste, your time, especially initially, when you have to learn how to operate it. Make sure you build into your work schedule the one day to 2 weeks learning time that you may need to gain mastery over it. At first, it may actually take more—not less—time to complete a task using the new technology, but over time it will probably save you time and even enhance the quality of your work as well.

When photocopying machines became common in office

buildings, for example, the need to make copies increased—and not just copies of documents that would have been carboned previously. New ways to use the copier emerged. Until employees learned the proper use of photocopying, they, or their assistants, were spending more time duplicating than before (even though it was now faster and easier).

But machines do not eliminate the people factor so crucial to success in business today. My research and observations make it clear to me that in business the best way to communicate is first in person, next, by phone, third, by E-mail, and, finally, by mail. Very soon videophones will become standard but, once again, even the ability to see the person you are speaking with on the phone does not replace the need to say hello, shake hands, and have the face-to-face observations technology will never replace.

Computers

If you use a personal computer, because power outages occur, or computers sometimes freeze or files get deleted unintentionally, take the time to back up your work, as you go along. Back up your data in multiple ways. Have a surge protector to reduce surge damage.

What About a Computer?

A best-selling novelist, when asked if he planned to get a computer (he has written on the same manual typewriter from the beginning of his career), replied, "No," he was not going to get one, but he might get one for his secretary. So, if your system is working, don't introduce new technology just because it's available. It just might cost you time.

How do you decide whether or not a computer is worth the money and time (to learn how to use the machine as well as the software) that getting one would mean to you and how you do your work? Here are some tasks that computers accomplish much more effortlessly than humans:

--repetitive typing, such as retyping the same words, paragraphs, or documents again and again.

--editing and revising copy such as rewriting a report or letter until you are pleased with the organization, length, or specific wording.

--creating charts to enhance your documents such as bar or line graphs or drawings.

--communicating with others via E-mail and the Internet.

--doing mathematical calculations or projections and estimates, including financial spreadsheets.

--the necessity of updating the same basic information on a regular basis, such as price lists, sell sheets, resumes, course overviews, bibliographies, or correspondence.

--creating and maintaining a database for reference or for mail merging correspondence to multiple recipients.

--sending fax transmissions from the computer.

--meeting specialized needs with specific software such as composing music, designing a building, doing desktop publishing of newsletters, magazines, or books.

--creating art work that can be stored or transmitted through the computer.

Computers, as everyone knows, are constantly being enhanced, updated, and outdated. Some opt to rent a computer, getting a newer model at the end of the rental agreement. Others prefer to buy, upgrading less frequently. Some companies have trade-in options built into their purchase agreements whereby you can trade in the current computer for a newer model in a certain period of time. Another option today is to have a computer custom built to your specifications for the amount of memory you need as well as whether or not there is a built in back-up system, and other technical considerations.

Certainly the software you use with your computer is as much a consideration for maximizing your efficiency as the computer itself. Not only should you select a software program suited to your individual needs but you need to take the time to master it so you feel confident about its nuances and subtleties. In addition to spending the time to train yourself by reading the manual or calling the help line of the software manufacturer for advice, you could hire a consultant to give you some time-saving tips or take a course.

E-mail and The Internet

E-mail, the ability to send and receive messages electronically through the Internet, as well as the other benefits of the Internet, such as the ability to quickly obtain research or visit the informational sites of magazines, book publishers, organizations, or businesses, are sometimes offset by the vast amounts of time these technological advances could consume if you are not careful.

It is even possible to get addicted to being "on line;" the immediate gratification and the very powerful pull and mesmerizing power of interacting instantly through E-mail could take up minutes or hours of the time you should be spending finishing up a priority project.

Because of the way the Internet ideally interacts in one seamless flow of information through search engines and key words, you could find just about anything. So unless you take control of the Internet, and how you spend your time on it, you could find yourself drifting further and further away from the original reason you went "on line" in the first place.

Similarly with e-mail, there is an expectation that e-mail will be returned instanteously even if you a) did not initiate the communication b) are busy doing other things c) only check your e-mail now and then or d) are inundated with literally 100+ messages daily, the majority unsolicited.

Once again, you have to establish clear guidelines for when, how, and if you will respond to your e-mails; for certain unsolicited e-mails, you might even want to develop an "auto responder" that you could automatically send back explaining why you will not immediately respond to the e-mail. If it is a communication you have not solicited, other instructions for why or how to communicate with you can be forwarded.

Whether it is the Internet in general or e-mail in particular, be aware of how long you are on line at all times. Some Internet providers will tell you, periodically, how long you are on line, but you should be aware of that time on your own as well.

You should also monitor whether you are on line, or sending or answering e-mail, by choice or by compulsion. Are you getting addicted to being on-line or are you carefully using these technological advances in the service of your time and work? (If you are getting addicted to the Internet, refer to the suggestions for conquering bad habits in Chapter 4 to help you overcome this problem.)

The Internet can also save vast amounts of time, however, especially for instant access to research material through such services as www.elibrary.com or daily newspapers or magazines that post articles or whole issues to the web. Through chat groups and special interest web sites, it is also possible to gather research by polling visitors on specific questions or even just reading and considering the concerns and information that they share.

Budget time for a "technology upgrade" hour, day, or week. Take the time to learn about your hardware equipment or software programs, as well as what is new and better that you could use. Go to trade shows, stop in computer stores, take courses, hire a consultant.

The Scanner

A scanner is a piece of equipment which enables you to scan images (art work, photographs, graphic designs) or text, with the addition of Optical Character Recognition (OCR) software. This revolutionary equipment, which is now available for less than $100 and is even part of a printer-fax-scanner combination machine, is definitely something most offices in the new millennium need to have. Scanning software enables you to edit images before you add it to the desktop publishing application of that image. "Hard copy" or text, instead of typing or typesetting it, can now be scanned and in that way put into a computer file for editing. This technology is revolutionizing entire industries, such as printing and graphic design, as well as writing and publishing.

The Fax Machine

This machine sends data over the phone lines and is definitely one of the key technological tools available today for saving time. For urgent communications, the fax machine eliminates the need for overnight delivery services. However, most agree that lengthy documents (more than 10 pages) should probably be sent by overnight mail unless the person receiving the fax has agreed that very long documents are okay to fax. Furthermore, fax transmissions sometimes go astray so you might want to check if your fax has been received. Plain paper fax machines are generally preferred in business because the fax transmissions are easier to read and will not fade in time.

Unsolicited fax transmissions are generally frowned upon in business as is faxing a resume (unless requested to do so.)

The Telephone

The telephone is a tool or a weapon, depending upon how you use it, or let it use you. Using the telephone for a long-distance phone interview may be the most important work-related task you accomplish on a given day; allowing numerous personal or business calls to interrupt you at crucial times when you are working may be frustrating, as well as time wasting.

Some workers allow personal calls at their offices only during a certain hour of the day, and only for a specified length of time. Others make it clear that personal calls, whenever they are received, must be brief and to the point, related to a specific question such as, "When do you expect us over tonight?" rather than just a way of "shooting the breeze."

If you're having trouble figuring out just how your telephone time is spent, or wasted, consider keeping a time log just for outgoing and incoming calls, noting the reason and duration of each call.

If you are prone to talk compulsively, set a time limit for your calls. Even if you're not, try to have a clear idea of what you want to say, and how long you will allow yourself to say it, whenever you initiate a call.

Secretaries, phone machines, and answering services can be helpful in making better use of the telephone, but only if used well. Most phone machines have monitors, so that you can screen calls and decide whether or not to pick up, without callers knowing you are there. Sometimes you may decide it is better to take a call since returning a call can entail even more time.

One of the few negatives related to most voice mail systems, however, is that you cannot monitor who is calling. If you decide you do not want to be interrupted, and the phone rings, once it goes to the voice mail system, you have to allow someone to leave a message in order to find out who is calling and why.

Some people find it useful to have categories of callers, or types of calls; on this list, personal and business contacts are classified into one of the categories—Always Put Through, Never Put Through, Always Take Message and Say I'll Return the Call. This system can be quite effective, since it eliminates that awkward interaction when a secretary says, "I'll check to see if she's in," and although the caller knows that the secretary is querying her boss, the secretary soon returns, saying, "No, I'm afraid she's not in at the moment, but she will return your call."

If you want to use the phone rather than letting it use you, consider memorizing, and using, this useful little phrase: "I can't talk right now." If you want, add "Can I get back to you?" Here are some other phrases to try if you have trouble getting off the phone, or telling the caller that you are unable to start a conversation:

> "I have to go now."
> "I can't talk much longer."
> "I have someone in my office."
> "I was just on my way out the door."
> "I have a staff meeting starting in a minute so we have to wrap this thing up."
> "Can't talk now, I have a roomful of people."

You may even find it necessary to make a list of friends whom you may dearly love but who have a telephone problem. These people engage in monologues, so it's rare that you can get off the phone in less than an hour. If you do want to call those kinds of friends, call them when you know they are unable to talk— just to give them a brief message or to stay in touch—or when you have plenty of time that you want to spend on the phone.

You should also consider some of the telephone devices that facilitate effective time management. For example, cordless phones permit you to walk around as you speak. This can be a great time saver if you find yourself saying "I'll call you back" because you need privacy; a cordless phone permits you to find that privacy all the time. Of course cell phones allow continual access even if on the train or in the car. Observe mobile phone etiquette by turning it off when in movie theatres, live performances, certain meetings or lectures, as well as safety concerns while driving or walking.

Phone machines or voice mail have become realities at work today. Decide if you will leave a message, or not. If you decide to leave one, speak clearly, slowly, and keep it short and to the point. If possible, leave a return phone number as well as the best time to reach you to avoid telephone tag. (Similarly, make the outgoing message on your machine or voice mail as explicit as possible.)

Here are other phone devices or available services or options to consider to increase your efficiency:

--call waiting

--caller ID (that allows you to see who's calling so you can decide if you will take the call or not; if you lose someone's phone number, you could also track it down through stored caller I.D.s, which could store as many as the last 25 names and phone numbers)

--call forwarding

--three-way or conference calling

--missed call (which, for a fee, allows you to put in a code and be connected to the call that you just missed)

--speed dialing

--speakerphone

last number redial (helpful if you keep getting a busy signal)

Use the phone creatively and avoid getting a reputation for only calling if you want to get something from someone. (One man I know is so used to being called for favors that he answers his phone by asking, "What can I do for you?") Once in a while, call business relations just to say hello. Listen to your business relation. You probably won't want to ask in great detail about the golf game last Saturday or the vacation in Spain, and you probably won't want to stay on more than a few minutes, but a sincere goodwill call may be welcome. The goodwill call suggestion, however, should be used with caution; you don't want to get a reputation for being a telephone time waster any more than you want to be known as an opportunist.

To keep track of calls and callers, instead of single slips of phone message sheets, it may be useful to have a central book, such as a spiral-bound one with a copy of each message. You will also be creating a permanent record of incoming callers, a handy record to have if you misplace a phone number a week or several months down the road. You can also take off the top sheet and give the message to someone but still have the permanent copy in the record book.

Dealing With Visitor Interruptions

In-person drop in visitors are as disruptive as telephone visitors who have, in effect, interrupted you with their call. You may be facile at handling both telephone and in-person interruptions but it is usually easier to get off the phone than to turn someone away who is right there in front of you. Without developing the reputation of being cold and aloof, you do want to establish rules for those you work with, namely, that drop-in visits should be avoided if possible. Get your co-workers or employees to develop the habit of calling first. (In some work situations this is impossible since you may work side by side.)

One technique to discourage drop-in visitors at the office, at least temporarily, is to have an established "quiet hour." You might put a sign on your door, "Do not disturb," or just let it be known that you are unavailable for one or more specific hours each day.

If drop-in visitors cannot be handled in other ways, try to deal with the immediate situation and get them out of your office as quickly as possible. Some executives purposely avoid having a chair in their office other than their own; discomfort (and the awkwardness of just standing there) may push visitors out faster than your words. If your drop-in visitor does not get the hint, especially if you have another appointment, come right out and say so. Obviously, if the drop-in visitor is your boss, more tact may be required to get him out, without encouraging his wrath. You might consider going in to see your boss, on a fixed or flexible basis, so drop-in visits to your office are minimized. In that way you might have more control over the situation, especially if you decide in advance what point or priority project you will be discussing.

If your job depends upon the social relations (and subsequent business) that may result from drop-in visits from customers or clients, such interruptions may not be time wasters for your job. If that is the case, you might, for instance, have a hot pot of coffee "on tap" as well as a comfortable sofa for your uninvited guests.

Each type of visitor interruption will be handled differently. Expected visitor interruptions should be planned for in advance with a written agenda for the meeting, any supporting materials that you will need to show or to distribute should be available.

If the visit is unexpected, you have to determine if it is desirable or intrusive. You could be in the midst of preparing a report for later that afternoon, but if the drop-in visitor is the senior vice president, you might want to stop what you're doing.

Time Off (Vacations, Sick Days, Personal Leave)

The right to shorter hours and longer vacations was achieved through the long efforts of laborers and union members. But no one, however, will make you take advantage of this extra time; it's up to you not just to take the time that's coming to you, but to plan the kind of activities that will be personally and professionally rewarding.

You might think you're saving money by puttering around the house, rather than going away, or saving time by not going away at all. Those who are self-employed often find it especially difficult to take a vacation; they are afraid that their business will deteriorate in their absence, or they are working on overlapping assignments and are unable to take time off during a project. If you can manage it, at least two weeks a year—two one-week vacations or one two-week vacation—will do wonders for your work abilities. It will also help you break the routine, focus on your health and emotional well-being, and allow you the time to renew intimate relationships.

If you can't get away for that length of time, consider what one advertising executive does. He divides his vacation time up throughout the year taking three or four-day mini-vacations with his wife, never traveling more than two hours by car from home.

Some workers may incorrectly fear that taking a vacation means possibly losing their job, but by failing to take one may create more stress and anxiety than by taking time off.

Experts agree that some time off from the job is a necessity for an employee's mental health and for family relationships that have so much influence on the worker's health and productivity.

If you get at least two weeks, your first vacation decision is whether you will take it consecutively, or split it up.

What is the best time to take your vacation? Some companies may require taking it when business is slow. Others may shut down and have company-wide vacations, making the decision for you. But if you do have some choice, pick the weeks that are best for you and your family. Since so many schedules at work will have to be coordinated, get your request in quickly to ensure your first or second favored periods.

There is also the "use it or lose it" policy that some companies follow. Some companies require vacation days to be taken within the calendar year, plus the first quarter of the next year. It is your responsibility to talk to a human resource manager or supervisor and find out what are the vacation policies at your company.

Here are some tips for making your vacation from work easier to take and more refreshing without anxiety about what you've left behind:

- Pick up some of the workload of a vacationing coworker or colleague so he or she will reciprocate when you are away.
- Right before your vacation (and afterwards), plan to put in late nights getting ahead (or caught up).
- If you really want to make sure you get away, be careful about new business that is offered to you in the weeks before your vacation if you would have to have it finished before your departure. Unless you are absolutely sure about your ability to meet, or beat, a deadline, try to either get a delayed deadline for this business, or refer it to a worthy colleague who will probably one day return the favor.
- Make sure a superior will know your vacation whereabouts. Designate someone that will call you if something happens at the office while you're away if something occurs that you should know about.
- Tell management what weeks you'd like to take off, but do your actual vacation dreaming or planning away from the job, and watch out for too much "we're going to .... on our vacation" bragging statements, or you may be seen as wasting company time with personal matters as well as being a braggart.
- Put effort into where you and your family would vacation best. Research and plan it, taking into account what you like to do and the cost. Plan something that matches your non-work interests, such as tennis camp, hiking or going on an archaeological dig. Sitting on a beach may help one person to unwind, but another might find it boring. There are many travel sites on the Internet to help you plan your vacation, such as www.Expedia.com.
- Even if money is a concern, take your vacation time anyway, if you need it, even if you don't go away on a trip.

Sick days and personal leave are other potential respites from work that you should use to your best advantage. As you learned in the section on obstacles to effective time management, employers are more sympathetic to absences because of physical ailments than emotional ones. You, however, are the best judge as to whether a day off this week might be to your advantage, and to your employer's.

Efficiency Breaks

Build into your workday the kind of rests that Elton Mayo found improved the efficiency of the workers at the Philadelphia textile mills in the 1920's. As Frances and Milbourn explain in their text, *Human Behavior in the Work Environment*, after efficiency experts and financial incentives for employees failed to reduce a 250 percent worker turnover rate, Mayo was called in for what became known as "The First Inquiry." Mayo discovered that permitting workers who stood all day to take four brief rest periods increased productivity and caused the turnover rate to drop.

As psychologist Dr. David Leeds says, "Even prizefighters get two minutes off between rounds."

Enhance your own work effectiveness, reduce fatigue, and decrease the possibility of making mistakes because of exhaustion by taking efficiency breaks or rests for five to thirty minutes, or an hour or longer, if necessary. Become atune to the timing and length of an efficiency break that will maximize your own work performance. Become sensitive to your physical or mental signals that it's time to break away. Note: use discretion in some work settings if your coworkers or employer might misinterpret your break as goofing off. Consider an exercise break, running for twenty minutes around lunchtime as one lawyer in Washington, D.C. does, or taking a walk; if necessary, find a way to take a brief nap.

Working With Others

Delegating

Do You Need Help Delegating More Effectively?

To find out if you could use help with delegating, ask yourself the following questions:

1. Are you working much longer hours than everyone around you, especially your subordinates?
2. Are you spending an inordinate amount of time each day on such easily "delegatable" tasks such as routine correspondence, non-priority phone calls, feeling yourself spread too thin?
3. Have you had an ulcer since taking this job, or felt as if you're heading for one?
4. Do you doubt you could select competent people to delegate to?
5. Do you dwell on past delegating disasters?
6. Are you a perfectionist?
7. Has anyone called you a "control freak"?
8. Are you unwilling to delegate the responsibility for the entire job, along with a specific task?
9. Have you ever fantasized that life could be more enjoyable if you could do *everything* yourself?
10. Have you come close to, or been, fired one or more times over the issue of delegating?

If you answer "yes" to one or more of the above questions, you probably need help with delegating.

Even though it may be harder for some to give up total control and delegate than others, the good news is that delegating well is a skill that can be learned. But first you have to recognize if you have a problem with delegating. Sure tip offs? Working excessively long hours. Second, not getting enough of the important stuff done --and you know what that is for your particular job or profession -- the projects, activities, or actions you should be doing. The activities that bring in sales, income, new customers or clients. The thinking stuff or even the client contact, if that's what you should be doing.

Delegating Effectively

Based on research and observations, here are the seven steps to becoming effective at delegating:

1. Decided what you will delegate.
2. Pick the right person to delegate to.

3. Unless proven otherwise, trust those to whom you delegate.
4. Give clear assignments and instructions.
5. Have definite "check points" for completion of a specific task or job and some system of on-going communication with those you delegate to.
6. Give credit to the person to whom you delegated.
7. Delegate responsibility for the job, not just one task.

1. Decide What You Will Delegate.

There are three considerations in deciding what to delegate:
1. Decide what is your priority task and delegate any tasks or jobs that stop you from focusing on that priority task. 2. Delegate what you can't do yourself because you don't have the skills or expertise. 3. Delegating what you won't do yourself because it's too boring, distracting from your priority task, or not the best use of your time. These are tasks that you could do, but you choose not to, because at this point in your career, someone else could do those jobs for you, such as routine correspondence or screening incoming calls.

2. Picking the Right Person to Delegate To.

Learn the traits and values, such as trust, and characteristics of those who will perform well when you delegate to them. A concern is whether or not someone is asking questions at the time a task is assigned. Listen and observe. As a North Carolina sales director notes, "You find out pretty quickly about people who are willing to take responsibility if they're already taking it on their own."

3. Trust Those You Delegate To.

Along with trust, you also have to grant the persons to whom you delegate the chance to do it their way. There is more than one acceptable way to do most tasks, but you do have the right to require that whatever you delegate is done accurately, and well.

4. Give Clear Assignments and Instructions.

Dr. Harry Levinson, chairman of the Levinson Institute in Boston, and a professor emeritus of psychology at Harvard Medical School, says that the fourth delegating step will especially help those managers who are resistant to delegating. Levinson advises:

> Learning to let go a little bit and trusting their people means giving them clear cut assignments with time boundaries, when they expect the assignments to be completed, and criteria for judging the quality of the work. Then reviewing each assignment, as it's completed, to see how well the person has done to help decide when he or she is ready for increased responsibility so that one let's go gradually.

Career consultant Nella Barkley, President of Crystal-Barkley Corporation, points out another pivotal part of giving clear assignments and instructions. As Barkley says:

> Learn how someone best receives information, whether they're your boss or your subordinate. Some receiving information best orally. For example, some CEOs, if you give them a ten page report, they'll never read it. [But] for some people, it's better to put it in writing first and let them think about it. You will generally learn how people receive information best by how they give information to you.

5. Have Definite Task Completion and a Follow-up System

Establish deadlines at the beginning of a specific project including several "mini-deadlines." In this way you may follow-up and check up on the work, especially till you are comfortable with someone's skills level, rather than waiting till the one deadline at the end.

6. Give credit.

You will inspire loyalty and a wish to serve in those you delegate to if you give them credit for their achievements. Too often those with a problem delegating will have someone do a task and then will complete the job themselves, taking all the credit. This strategy eventually backfires, however, since taking all the credit develops a bad feeling among coworkers and subordinates.

7. Delegate Responsbility for the Job, Not Just the Task.

There are three issues at the bottom of a failure to delegate responsibility for the job, not just one task. The first is that you must trust those you delegate to will do a good job. Second, and this is hard for high achievers, the ones most likely to have a problem delegating, to do: you have to be willing to accept the fact that the person you delegate to may do the job worse or, heaven forbid, even better than you. Third, you have to be willing to help them learn from their mistakes, if they make them.

Only by delegating entire jobs, not just tasks, will you avoid the monkey-on-the-back syndrome, first espoused in the classic *Harvard Business Review* article, "Management time: Who's got the monkey?" Co-authors and management consultants William Oncken, Jr. and Donald L. Wass, step by step, show how managers who fail to delegate responsibility as well as tasks will eventually find themselves reporting to their subordinates, and doing some of *their* work, rather than vice versa!

Here are five additional rules for delegating provided by Letitia Baldrige, etiquette expert and former social secretary to the White House during the Kennedy administration:

1. I still think the way to get someone to cooperate with you is to be sensitive to his or her time problems:
First, you say how desperate you are. Second, you ask nicely. Third, you state for exactly how long you're going to need this person and what the duties will be.
2. Encourage the person during the operation, particularly if it's more work, and it's taking longer, than you thought.
3. Never be so busy and arrogant yourself that you don't take time to praise.
4. After you've delegated the authority and the job is done, be sure to go on record giving credit to those who did a

terrific job. That is very important. Then they'll be ready to work for you again... fast.

5. To ensure permanent-delegation, education comes into it. You may have to bring the person up to speed. That may require giving him or her a special book to read, suggesting a six-week course at night, or just getting a subscription to a trade publication that will make him more sophisticated about his job.

Whether you work with others, or alone, delegating can dramatically increase how effectively you manage your time. (If you delegate improperly, it can be an enormous time drain.) Delegating—giving up total control of your work and entrusting certain tasks to others—is hard for some workers, yet the inability to delegate often undermines your own, or your company's, growth and profits.

If you have a problem delegating, try to analyze where it stems from: Do you need to control everything in your work environment? Do you doubt you could hire someone competent? Have you had bad prior experiences with delegating so you are afraid to try it again? Are you fearful someone else can do it better than you?

You can delegate to another worker or to a machine, a robot or a word processor, for example, or to a service, such as a printing firm that will do addressing and envelope stuffing. Delegating is not the same thing as passing the buck. You are paying someone to perform some of your tasks to free yourself to perform others, usually more important and specialized, ones. Company presidents, who started a firm from scratch, may still be fixing machines when their time would be better spent planning and inventing. By contrast, in large bureaucracies, being given the power to delegate is seen as a status symbol; the more people that work for you, the more important you must be. Delegating well can lead to increased efficiency; delegating badly— misusing your power—can lead to poor employee relations. For example, it may be tempting to ask your secretary to play baby-sitter; in the long run, it may be more efficient to line up a student you call on just for that purpose.

Working with Superiors

Being overly familiar, or too close-mouthed, can cause problems in working with superiors. If you over-involve your superiors in what you are doing—at work or in your personal life—you may be wasting valuable time that could be spent actually working, or make your superior feel burdened by your own personal affairs (and wondering if you can take care of things). If, by contrast, you fail to keep your boss informed about your work, she may falsely believe you are unproductive. Moderation is the key; neither "all talk, no action" nor "all action, no talk" are desirable extremes.

Let's say you are in charge of a specialized reference collection maintained in a college library. Although somewhat autonomous, you were hired by the senior librarian, and she wants to be informed of your activities. You could keep her informed by writing a weekly, bi-weekly, or monthly memo. You could decide a more informal approach is what's needed— updating her over coffee or lunch every so often. Unless your superiors issue guidelines on how and when to update them on your work—and often they do not—it is up to you to devise, and follow through on, an effective plan. Even if you decide the more casual approach is what's needed, it should not be casual for you.

What about socializing outside of the office? Use your discretion. You may think it would aid your office relationship to meet outside of the job. You may decide it would be best to let your boss make the first move. A circumstance might arise, such as an extra pair of tickets to a concert or sports event that you know he'd enjoy, that would naturally lend itself to after-work socializing. Timing, and the personalities involved, should be taken into account on a job by job, situation by situation basis.

Compulsive Talkers

Beware the compulsive talker! Compulsive talkers waste their time, and will gladly waste yours, if you let them. Compulsive talkers take energy away from their work and put it into talking about their work.

If you have a compulsive talking problem, consider maintaining a written daily journal as a way of diverting your output away from those around you. (At the least, you will be saving *them* time.) Maybe you will have to talk into a tape recorder just to get over your need to talk compulsively, or seek professional help to find out what motivates the constant chatter.

What's behind compulsive talking? Muriel Schiffman, author of *Self Therapy* and *Gestalt Self Therapy*, describes two types of compulsive talkers, and their motivations:

> 1. This talker has a dark secret. Talking in this instance is a red herring, like the mother bird who distracts you and tries to lead you away from the baby birds.... He is also trying to atone for years of secrecy by "telling all" now (about something else).... This kind of talker is often entertaining if exhausting.
>
> 2. This talker has never had anyone to listen to him at some important period in his life.... Since a neurotic is someone who never got what he needed in the beginning, he never learned how to get it. So this deprived talker sets himself up again and again to be rejected; he is very boring.

Is there a cure? Schiffman, who had this problem herself, stopped talking compulsively. How? "I sublimated my pattern by lecturing three nights a week and sometimes, by special invitation, from ten am. to six p.m.... Eventually, after many, many therapy sessions which uncovered innumerable facets to my unconscious motivations, I lost the desire to lecture at all as well as the craving to talk too much."

Working Too Much

Are you addicted to work? Would you rather work than do anything else? Are you at work early in the morning, into late hours on weekday nights, as well over the weekends, or even on vacations? Do you even allow yourself to take a vacation? Do you have trouble stopping work once you get started?

Workaholics are perfectionists and high energy people; being around them, or working for or with them, places demands on others that they may not meet. Like alcoholism, workaholism is a hard addiction to cure since work has become a way of avoiding other issues. Furthermore, since there is such an emphasis on the work ethic, many may fail to see their excessively-long hours at work as a negative. When does working hard, a positive value, become workaholism, an addiction that can cause stress and burnout?

"I use my work to avoid socializing," says Kathy, 32, an analyst for a stock brokerage firm. Saturday nights, when she might be out on a date, Kathy is home, rereading financial newspapers.

Workaholism is actually a time waster in disguise. The basis of workaholism is the mismanagement of work and personal time. If the workaholic planned his or her time better, he or she might not need to pull as many "all nighters" to get the work done. Too much of anything, including work, is rarely beneficial to a person's overall well-being, physical, mental, intellectual, emotional, and social. Workaholics, oblivious of the schedules that others adhere to, may even be found working on weekends, Christmas Eve, or other holidays —along with their dutiful employees.

For additional discussion about "Types You May Encounter in Work-Related Situations," see Chapter 9 in my book, *Business Protocol*, covering 17 different types including the manipulator, the spy, the braggart, and the hidden agendist.

Making the Most of Meetings

The daily, weekly, or monthly meeting can be a notorious time waster. Yet, if used correctly, it can also be a time saver. For example, you can use meetings to learn about your company, or your project, so you become aware of new trends.

Here are suggested guidelines for conducting meetings:

1. Make sure there is a reason for the meeting and that all those expected to attend have been advised, in writing, of that purpose as well as the time the meeting will start and finish. Make it clear in your advance notices that the meeting will start on time and that it is important to be on time, not late.
2. Stick to the starting time; latecomers will get the point at least for the next meeting and those who are on time will not be kept waiting for the few latecomers.
3. Have a written agenda for the meeting and follow it.
4. Decide in advance if you, or someone you delegate to, will take notes during the meeting. If you decide to tape record the meeting, make provisions for transcribing the tape.
5. Keep discussions to the topic at hand and control questions that get off on a tangent or your meeting (and you) may start to seem unfocused and disorganized.
6. Be certain that, by the end of the meeting, participants have a sense of accomplishment. Summarize what the meeting achieved, if necessary.
7. Decide in advance if you will followup the meeting with a written synopsis of what was accomplished.
8. End on time.
9. Thank participants for attending and advise them if they will receive a written or oral follow up. If there will be another meeting, announce when it will take place.

If you have to attend a meeting, avoid saying anything just because you want to brag about the work you are doing, as a way of gaining recognition. If you have something specific to contribute, or a pertinent question to ask, by all means speak up. Make notes in advance so that whether you make a statement or ask a question, you present your ideas or questions succinctly and tactfully.

If you attend conferences, set yourself clear goals. If someone else is sending you there, you may be required to write a report detailing what you gained from it. If you do write such a report, keep it simple and clear. You may want to go on for fifteen pages, but you may be wasting the time of the person who has to read it, and your time in creating such a detailed report. Even if you are not asked to set goals, or to write a report, do it for yourself. Before attending any meeting or conference, have a clear idea what you want to get out of it.

Exhibiting at a trade show requires far more planning, effort, and resources than most first-timers realize. If you do plan to exhibit at a trade show, try to "walk the show" the year before you plan to exhibit, noting the kinds of displays that are exhibited as well as what the best position is for your table or booth. If you do not have that much advance time available to you, ask to see a floor plan of the exhibit hall. Also request the names of at least three other individuals or companies that are similar to yours that exhibited before whom you might call for information and guidelines.

Exhibitor is a monthly trade publication devoted to the exhibiting field. There are also experts that you might contact who consult just on making the most of a trade show exhibiting experience.

Improving Communication at Work

Communication in work situations may involve two persons (dyadic), three persons (triadic), four or more persons (social network). There are elements that are unique to each type of interaction. A dyad, say you and your boss, has the potential for greater intimacy (and confidentiality). It also is less secure since it depends on both members for its maintenance but only one for its dissolution. A triad is easier to maintain since the third member serves to perpetuate the group. It is, however, less intimate since secrecy is less assured than in a dyad. A network of four or five, such as a typing pool, has the potential for hundreds of interrelationships. Relationships may be more superficial than in a dyad or triad, but easier to maintain.

Communication at work may be improved by understanding the nature of your work relationships (whether they are dyadic, triadic, or networks), basics about communication skills, and certain complexities of social relationships that may inhibit good communication. For example, the self-fulfilling prophesy means that your self-perception, even if negative, you unwittingly make it come true. Thus if you see yourself as competent and able to relate well at the office, it becomes true. Conversely, if you see yourself as someone who has trouble communicating with your superiors or peers and is insecure, that may also become true.

Therefore it is paramount that you have a good self-image and self-esteem; it will enhance your relationships and communication at work. Improve your self-image by creating a positive progressive spiral. In *Dyadic Communication*, Wilmot describes it: "the actions of the individual supply a multiplier effect in reinforcement. The better you do, the more worthwhile you feel; the more worthwhile you feel, the better you do."

Two communication inhibitors that Wilmot cautions against are paradoxes and double binds. A paradox is a contradictory statement such as the following:

> Ignore this sign

A double bind is a type of paradox in which a nonverbal message contradicts a verbal one. For example, you come to work looking exhausted. When your boss asks if you've been working too hard, you answer, "No, I've never been more rested." But your appearance contradicts your statement and places your boss in a double bind.

You cannot control how your boss, subordinates, or coworkers talk to you but you can control your own verbal and nonverbal behavior. Since it is a fact of interpersonal relationships that communication is usually reciprocal— people respond to you as you respond to them and vice versa—through your own behavior you do have some control. If you have a good self-image and avoid paradoxes and double binds, you have a better chance of inspiring better communication at work.

Since communication is reciprocal, avoid telling your boss or subordinates information that it would be inappropriate for them to tell you in kind. Take a long view of work relationships rather than trying to come on too strong and too fast.

WORK GOALS
Long-range Planning

People who fail to manage their time efficiently are usually unable to set and maintain long-range goals. They let the daily work ups and downs interfere with accomplishing their primary goals. Consider your long-range career goals. Where do you want to be in five years? Ten years from now?

Starting to think in terms of objectives to accomplish will make it easier for you to prioritize. Some experts feel that few people are able to handle more than three work-related goals simultaneously. (Some people find they can only handle one!) Within each goal, however, there may be dozens or hundreds of small steps that you have to take. (You may wish to refer to pages 10-11, Creative Time Management Principle #2 - Setting Goals.)

Progress Reports

People who mismanage their time usually need help setting *realistic* daily goals. Breaking a large task up into daily tasks is the foundation of good time management. If you feel overwhelmed by how large your goal is—writing a book, getting a degree, giving a speech, completing a study, selling x number of tractors, or designing an employee manual—break it down into daily goals. You may find that by tackling, and achieving, a manageable task—"Today I will call seven sales prospects" or "Today I will read sixty pages"—you will feel a sense of accomplishment.

Reward yourself for achieving each daily goal. Use any remaining time to achieve another goal (or improve what you've done.)

Progress reports may be only for your boss; a personal progress report might give you the daily feedback that you need to manage your time better. Jerry, an aspiring novelist, bought a diary solely to list the activities he accomplished that day, even if it was just

"Spent three hours thinking about the plot of my novel." In that way, he began to see that the time he thought he was wasting— because he didn't have any manuscript pages to show for it— he actually had used wisely. Even though it took him two years to finish the novel, entering into his diary "Wrote twenty pages today" made the task more manageable than focusing on "How am I ever going to write four hundred enthralling pages?"

Consider creating or purchasing daily progress sheets to keep track of your accomplishments (or your time). Here's a sample of an activity sheet with some of the categories filled in:

Work Sheet	Date Tuesday, June 2	
Hours	Activity	Accomplished
9 am-11 am	Phone calls. Accepted lecture.	
	Returned calls from yesterday.	
11am-12	Correspondence	Answered 5 letters.
12-1 pm	Lunch Read *Wall Street Journal*	
1-3 pm	Staff Meeting	
3-5 pm	Dictating notes on meeting.	
5-7 pm	Commuting. Reading magazines.	

Your activity/accomplishment log need not be divided up by time periods; one man has his day divided up into these four categories: Work; Chores; Exercise; and Relaxation. Within his own categories, he lists what he's accomplishing that day.

It's important not just to do what you have to do right now, but to follow up. Do you check up on projects, memos, or telephone calls that have not been returned? Do you let too much time—or not enough—elapse between starting and completing a job-related function? Are you projecting an image that will further, or hinder, your career?

In *Getting Things Done*, Edwin C. Bliss advises that right after a project has been completed, while the experience is still fresh in your mind, especially if you have been dissatisfied with the outcome, write yourself a brief appraisal. Note what you learned from that project. Date it and keep it for later review.

Measuring Your Success

The Hawthorne Effect, discovered by Elton Mayo when he was conducting an experiment on the effect of levels of illumination on worker productivity at an electric company in the late 1 920's and early 1930's, shows why measuring your success is important. Mayo found that workers in the control group (who did not have any changes made in their lighting) showed increased productivity; at the same time, whether lights were dimmed or brightened, those in the experimental group showed increased productivity. The phenomenon, known as the Hawthorne Effect, meant this: just the act of being studied or measured led to increased productivity.

You can draw your own conclusions as to whether this increase was due to the need to impress the researcher (employed by management) or because of the favorable human response to being noticed and cared about. Generally, you are not evaluated daily by others. Is there a way you can employ the Hawthorne Effect to your advantage? Daily logs will help; no one can observe you more intimately than you, yourself.

Managing your time at work well means figuring out what you have to do, and doing it, as quickly and effectively as possible.

There are many ways of measuring success—in dollars and cents, by promotions, peer approval, or in public recognition.Whatever your measures for success, make them concrete so you'll know when you've achieved them.

In the next chapter we will look at finding "hidden" time as well as how all the concepts discussed in this book thus far can be applied to a variety of work-related situations, such as the "nine-to-fiver" or executive traditional worker, the self-employed or freelancer, small business owners, the creative person, and others.

7
Applying
Creative Time Management

Time is the most valuable thing a man can spend.
        THEOPHRASTUS (?-278 B.C.)

The concept of time

Time is a cultural concept. Westerners, for example, think in terms of twenty-four hours in a day, and seven days in a week. However, those divisions are arbirtrary. There is no such thing as "a week;" we have created that concept. Time is an idea that varies greatly from culture to culture, within each culture, and even between individuals. The workday, for example, will differ for an office worker in Manhattan, for whom it may start at nine, and for one in Lima, Peru, for whom it may begin before eight. Teachers and students view time away from classrooms during the summer months far differently than typical workers who are still in their offices, although in some countries, such as France, the entire month of August may be vacation time for workers, or in the United States, for some occupations, such as psychiatrists and psychologists, as well.

MAKING PRODUCTIVE USE OF YOUR "HIDDEN" TIME

"Hidden" time is time that you previously mismanaged, consumed with distractions, or used for other tasks or activities, that you turn into productive time for pursuing your priority tasks. What are your "hidden" times? Think about your average workday, weekday evening, or free day. Is there time you might reorganize into your "hidden" concentrated time? If necessary, create time logs and analyze how you spend your time. Identify any "hidden" times.

Hidden time may be moments or minutes that you turn into productive use just as much as blocks of time you structure in to your day. For example, you might use the five minutes you usually spend waiting for the bus, or the half hour waiting in someone's office, to plan, dictate, read, work on your laptop computer, return or receive calls on your cell phone, or just relax and meditate.

Your hidden time may also change from month to month, or year to year. When my second son was three, since I did not want to hire a daytime sitter, I soon realized unless I found "hidden" time it would be years before I had blocks of work time. I discovered that if I forced myself to wake up by 4 a.m., I could work uninterrupted until at least 7 a.m. Even though my children are much older now so I have schooltime to work uninterrupted, I still enjoy my "hidden" time for concentrated work on a priority project.

Daydreaming represents another potential opportunity for creating additional productive "hidden" time. Tim Walsh, vice president of marketing and product development for Patch Products, began a whole new career because of daydreaming. Says Walsh: "In 1989 I was working at a rehabilitation center for post-operative back patients. They would be on the treadmill or in the whirlpool and I had time to kill." That time provided him with the opportunity to daydream about a game he and his friends at college had thought up. Walsh went on to switch careers to become a game developer producing the game, TriBond® which has sold over 1.5 million units, as well as numerous other products.

USING YOUR ENERGY HIGHS AND LOWS

Another way to improve the way you plan and schedule a day is to become aware of your personal energy highs and lows. No two persons have the same biological rhythms--your neighbor may thrive on five hours of sleep a night but you feel like a zombie unless you get at least eight.

A primary consideration in planning and scheduling your day is, therefore, whether you are a morning, afternoon, or evening type of person (or some combination of the three). Try to plan your time within your own energy cycles. Another concern is how much sleep you really need. You may need ten hours, or only five; there is no absolute rule about needing eight hours a day.*

Another notion that will help you apply creative time management to your work and leisure time is something Flora Davis, author of *Living Alive!*, and others refer to as the postprandial dip---the period, sometime after lunch and in the afternoon, when someone "just runs out of steam," as Davis says. When psychologists have studied this phenomnon, they found that fifty percent of their subjects experienced postprandial dip. The term, however, is deceptive since researchers have found that postprandial dip has nothing to do with when (or if) you have lunch. What is important to know is that one out of two persons seems to experience a postprandial dip. If you are one of them, plan and schedule your day with that afternoon energy low in mind. Davis, for example, since she has a postprandial dip that is quite late-- between four and five in the afternoon, she tries "not to read something heavy and dull because, on the spot, it's going to put me to sleep." A self-employed freelance writer, in the summertime, Davis will go swimming between four and five "because it wakes me up." In the wintertime, she'll use that time to go grocery shopping. If you work in a regular outside office, your postprandial dip might be an excellent time to do filing, return phone calls, or plan an outside meeting so you force yourself to keep moving.

*For an extensive discussion of sleep and sleep-related issues such as sleep need, sleep deprivation, and fatigue, see *The Encyclopedia of Sleep and Sleep Disorders*, by Michael J. Thorpy, M.D. and J. Yager, Ph.D., New York: Facts on File, 1991.

STRUCTURING TIME

Won't it all work out somehow if you can just "muddle through"? Stop and think for a minute. As the demands on your time have changed in your life, have you adjusted your time budget to reflect those changes? Do you even have a time budget? Perhaps you have just had a child, have a vacation coming up in a week, or you're just gotten a promotion. Did you, to accommodate those changes, shift your activities? Maybe it was not so recently that a change occurred--you got promoted, you switched jobs, your friend moved out-of-town--but are you still managing your time the same old way?

Or maybe you're just sick and tired of always being "busy" but rarely accomplishing anything that means that much to you. It may just be that you don't want to have to apologize again for having to cancel a meeting with a friend, or to keep a valued customer waiting.

Changing circumstances dictate altering how you manage your time. Your primary work role may be that of executive, but your family relations and community activities are other roles that demand your time. Few of us play only one role; how best to perform each role is a key theme when planning your time. You may be an accountant, paid by the hour, with numerous outside obligations, or a self-employed researcher, paid by the project, who is active in sports and culture activities.

But time is relative: a 76-year- old retired grandmother may feel she has less time and is more rushed than her 33-year-old married granddaughter, working full-time and taking care of two toddlers, with her multiple obligations.

This chapter deals with structuring time for various roles; read the section that only pertains to you or read each section since you might benefit from applying those suggestions as well.

For "Nine-to-fivers" or Executive Time

Few people today are exactly "nine-to-fivers" since "start-up" time—getting dressed, having breakfast, commuting back and forth—can aid or interfere with actual work time as much as how early you get to the office, how late you stay, and how much "after hours" studying, entertaining, or traveling you are expected to do.

Those in formal settings may benefit even more from stringent self-checks, since much work may be so routinized one could mistakenly believe that providing one's physical presence is equivalent to working. Your boss may tell you to do a report, and then ask you to do six other things. You let the report slide, complete the other things, and when she asks for that report, you say you need a little more time to polish it, and then write it in a hurry.

The telephone may be your biggest help, and your greatest annoyance. As the treasurer of a 550-employee freight company put it: "We have come full circle. Before the phone it was difficult to reach someone. With voice mail, we have the same problem."

To get around this, be as explicit as possible in your voice mail, or with your secretary, as to when and how someone could reach you. A specific time, such as "I'll be back from my meeting by eleven tomorrow morning" or "Call after four p.m." will be more likely to reduce telephone tag than a general greeting without any useful details.

If you work in a structured traditional office setting, try to pinpoint the uninterrupted work periods available to you, e. g., from arrival to lunch or from after lunch till departure. Then, except for necessary interruptions, use those blocks of work time to concentrate and accomplish your short- and long-term goals. Try to reserve fifteen minutes at the end of each day to review that day's "to do" list, noting where you achieved your goals, where you fell short, and setting your priorities for the next day. As we've seen, it may be counterproductive to your job, or to your personal needs, to frequently need to work outside your office. Trains, chaotic family rooms, and rooms where dinner parties are in progress are family rooms, and rooms where dinner parties are in progress are not the most conducive places to work efficiently. Good planning should minimize the frequency with which this occurs.

Remember, unrealistic deadlines should be revised well in advance of any due dates. You have to be as clear as possible about what deadlines you are capable of meeting. But you also do not work in a vacuum. Sometimes it is management, not you, that is guilty of imposing impossible deadlines.

Sometimes the best way to get the most work done at the office is to work around traditional office hours. That's what the 39-year-old vice president at a manufacturing company in Connecticut does: he arrives each day by 8:15, and leaves by 4:30, but since his secretary and everyone else has left by 3:45, he finds his most productive time is after 4 o'clock. "At that time in the afternoon, the phone calls are not that frequent. I'm the last one here and I'm not getting troubleshooting problems so one hundred percent of my concentration is on my own work. Prior to that I have to split my concentration up between my job and things that are going on in the plant."

He also stays productive by avoiding doing too many things at once. Instead, he will do one job for the entire morning, and another job in the afternoon. That way he avoids "trying to do three or four things at once, which can be stressful."

The biggest time waster at his company? "Petty arguments between employees" that require him to take time to be a referee. (They have 75 employees but do not have a personnel director whose job it would be to deal with such disputes.)

For others, especially working mothers with small children, the best way to organize the traditional workday nontraditionally through flexible hours, part-time, or working some hours or days "on site" and others "at home." For 33-year-old Marilyn, the conference coordinator at a New York college, working three days a week has been the best solution since she has two daughters, ages three and five months. She explains why this is the "best set up both personally and professionally" for her: "[Working three days a week] allows me great flexibility and also super time management. I can say honestly that I enjoy my leisure time at home (though raising kids isn't exactly leisurely) and I enjoy the challenges of work."

Although most are concerned that working part-time can derail a career, a two-year study by Purdue University researcher Shelley MacDermid and Mary Dean Lee, of McGill University in Montreal, found that for the 87 corporate professionals and managers that they studied, working less than full-time had not been detrimental to their career advancement. Ninety percent of the women, were reported to be happier with the reduced work load, and three out of four spouses said the arrangement was a success for the family.

But not all jobs lend themselves to reduced work loads, nor could the woman or family absorb the reduction in salary that usually follows. A married mother of three children, ages five months to five years, whose family needs her second income, manages to work fulltime as an advertising executive. How does she do it all? I asked. She replied: "I focus on three things: getting kids fed, in and out of the house, and in and out of bed. Everything else gets forgotten."

Best-selling author Harvey Mackay, who is also the CEO of the $85 million Mackay Envelope Corporation, devotes a short chapter to time management in his latest book, *Pushing the Envelope*. Mackay notes that he first learned the importance of being on time from his father, who was an Associated Press correspondent. His father used to say, "Miss a deadline, miss a headline."

The theme to all of Mackay's time management tips are that to be successful you should take control of your time and not let it slip through your fingers: you don't get sales from other salesmen but from customers; spend your time with them; work twice as hard as everyone else; use whatever technology, such as a car phone, or service, such as a valet service, to save the precious time available to you.

For the Self-Employed and Freelancers

Although being self-employed carries the connotation of working "for yourself," virtually all self-employed workers are dependent upon clients, patients, patrons, and similar fee-generating income sources. Sometimes being self-employed can place greater restrictions on freedom than working for a single employer (whether another individual or a huge conglomerate.) For many self-employed persons, obtaining work can involve as much time and effort as doing it. By contrast, the traditional nine-to-fiver, by the very nature of the work structure, usually has work "handed" to him.

If you are self-employed, you should rate yourself as an employer. Do you have a pension plan, vacation time, sick days, time for personal leave, maternity leave? If someone else employed you, you'd certainly expect some of those benefits. Don't drive yourself into an unpensioned grave for the seeming luxury of self-employment; you might turn out to be the worst employer you've ever had. Self-employment can mean increased freedom in your daily affairs; it can also mean increased pressure, fewer hours with your friends and family, and little financial security. It may be harder for you to find the time to perform your skill, or create your product, if you are unable to delegate the busywork that would fall on someone else's shoulders if you were in a corporate environment with extensive support services.

A consultant, so involved with handling her current clients that she does not spend time adding new clients or keeping up with previous ones, may find her business begins to suffer.

Creative and effective time management may make or break a self-employed person. Bob, 53, a self-employed counselor, says, "I feel more pressure because I know that the temptation to just sit down and watch TV or to lie in bed till ten o'clock in the morning is very great and there's no one there to say, 'Hey, get up and punch a time clock.'"

Adhering to a fixed schedule, with provisions for overtime, seems to be the time management technique of choice for those who are self-employed in creative professions. Jack, 67, a successful self-employed nonfiction writer for over 40 years, writes: "The *only* way to become successful at free-lancing is to run your operation like a business.... Hit your desk at specific hours. Otherwise the tendency to goof off will take over.... Be prepared, too, for overtime work. There will be times when deadlines must be met, and hence night work and weekend work will be necessary."

Factors that affect time management for the self-employed are: where you work (in your home or "outside"); the pattern of work (at a desk or traveling most of the time); and the nature of work (whether a skill or a product). A psychotherapist with an outside office and a secretary, for example, may sit in a room most of the day with patients coming to see her. The therapist will have a structure imposed on her by the presence, and schedule, of her secretary and clients. It will be more difficult for her to "goof off" than it might be for a self-employed artist who works alone at home. An actor who earns his living making TV commercials may spend eight hours "out on call," with four of those hours spent "waiting" for appointments, or between auditions. He may have to be more disciplined during periods when there are no auditions or parts to be had since he probably does not have an outside "office."

Maximizing efficient communication is especially important for the self-employed. Whether or not you even get a job may depend upon promptly receiving, or returning, phone calls. Here is the suggestion from the president and CEO of one-person consulting company for enhancing communication: "Each person should establish a personal communication protocol to optimize contacts and communicate that via each channel. For example, "Please contact me most reliability via e-mail, unless it is urgent, where voice mail should be used. Please confirm transmission success for attachment via e-mail, and use fax to ensure receipt if there is any question or uncertainty."

Self-employed persons who work at home create solutions to the " how to get going in the morning when you don't commute to work" situation. Brian, 59, a self-employed labor mediator who works at home, begins his day by walking his dog, buying the newspaper, and reading it over breakfast. Unless he has an outside appointment, he begins each workday by nine, as if he just arrived at corporate headquarters.

A factor for those who are self-employed to consider is a phenomenon that I call *time lag*. Let's say that right now you've got more work than you can handle. You might feel your problem is not having enough time to do all the work that's coming your way. Think again. " I was right at the end of finishing a book I had worked on for the past two years when a big newspaper called me," said Arlene, a woman in her forties who writes articles and books. "The editor needed an article, and I said I couldn't do it because I was finishing my book. I told her I'd give her a call when I was free." A few months later, when Arlene was free, she called, but the editor wouldn't take her call. Now Arlene had the time, but couldn't find editors who wanted her time—a classic example of time lag.

The reason that the self-employed have the problem of time lag is difficulty in looking past what they are currently doing, and planning ahead so that something is "in the pipeline," and ready to be started when the current work is completed. The worst time to get work—whether it's a job or a new assignment—is when you're not working. Those who are self-employed have to force themselves to devise basic time management principles to fit their specific needs, such as x, y, and z (future objectives) must be pursued while a and b (current objectives) are ongoing.

Avoiding time lag if you are self-employed requires sharp judgment as to how long a given project will actually take—not how long you'd like it to take. That way you can give yourself or your client a realistic deadline (starting *and* ending) for the next project, whether for two weeks or two years.

You might find it useful to create an organized system for keeping track of your assignments, as well as any potential projects that you are currently circulating or proposing. Try using the "ABC" approach of (A) What You Have, (B) What you Want, and (C) Getting What You Want By Using (A) and (B). Using cards or notebooks, apply the "who, what, where, when, how, why" analysis.

Here's one example of the kind of system you might devise:

```
Sample Card for Keeping Track of Assignments
Project Description:
Client contact information:
      (Name, title, company, address, phone, fax, E-mail)
Preferred way to contact:
Date Assigned:                    Due Date:
Length/Type:
Fee:
Budget:
Expenses:
Submitted On:
Follow-up:
Outcome:
```

For the Creative Person

Guard your creativity as you would guard the most precious diamond in the world!

Protect those moments of inspiration with the respect and reverence that each one deserves. There are numerous examples throughout history of just how delicate true creativity can be, as the writer creates an entire novel just from the dream she remembers upon awakening, the artist paints a nightmare, or the poet finds the words "pouring out" and on to the page, words that come as fast and furiously as never before, only to stop coming again for years or ever more after that intense creative moment.

You cannot force creativity but you can, by creating the right conditions for it, help foster it. (By the same token, you can stop it in its tracks by doing the opposite of these suggestions.)

Here, then, are some ways to save time for the creative person by inspiring additional creative output:

• Keep a pad near your bed so if you have a dream or a nightmare, you can quickly write it down before forgetting it.

• Try, as much as possible, to block out concentrated time periods when you work and don't let anything or anyone mail system take calls. Even shut off the radio if that distracts you.

- Avoid people whose negativity or criticism shuts down your creative juices.
- Don't show what you're working on too soon or to too many people until you are completely finished.
- Clear up enough in your external environment that your inner creativity is not distracted by the clutter.
- Try to focus on only one project at a time, physically removing other creative pulls from your visible environment.
- Trust your instincts and your sensibilities.
- Date and organize your creative projects so you don't get confused as to what versions or drafts you wish to keep and which ones you wish to discard. (When in doubt, hold on to your creative products. Store it in a closet, file it away. You can always throw something out but some creative efforts, once destroyed, can never be redone or restored.)
- Surround yourself with people who respect your creative spirit and process. Train your children, spouse, and friends to understand how interruptions can cause your creative effort – even your words – to vanish.

Those are some suggestions for enhancing the creative process itself. But there is another way most creative persons needs to learn to spend his or her time, however, and that is with the business end of their creative career. Too many creative people fear that being actively involved in doing even some of the numerous business-related concerns and details of running a business will completely obliterate their creative time. Fearing that, they do nothing at all. As a result, the business end of being creative, including marketing, sales, customer relations, and promotion, gets too little of their time, or none at all, so that the creative person's career suffers in the short- or long-run.

Of course having an excellent manager, or delegating certain tasks to a publicist, marketing, selling, or direct mail company, will help, but the creative person will still need to do a part of the business part of being creative.

Perhaps the best solution is to apply the 80/20 rule: spend 80% of your time creating, and 20% of your time doing the business part of your career. If you start focusing only on the business part, not only will you be frustrated but within a short period of time you will no longer have new creative products to sell.

If you focus only on the creative part, not only will your records be in disarray but you will never become, or will cease being, a business. However, for many, perhaps most, creative people, that's okay. They have managers or agents to handle the business concerns.

The key point to share is that creative people truly are in a different category than business owners or executives. Creative people think differently and, therefore, approach getting organized, or staying organized, as well as how they manage their time in a unique way.

Creative people have to walk the fine line among the time pulls of productive work, often done in isolation, which usually enables them to create, doing the business aspect of their career, as well as interacting with others, often difficult during the hours or even the days or months of intense concentration on absorbing creative projects.

Two popular books that deal just with time management and creative people are Lee Silber's *Time Management for the Creative Person* and Dorothy Lehmkuhl and Dolores Lamping's *Organizing for the Creative Person*.

For Small Business Owners

The advice for small business owners is similar to that of the creative person or freelancer but the difference is that the small business owner has to be responsive to every single customer. The creative person or freelancer is usually more concerned with creating product and with the client who hired him or her than with individual customers. The small business owner is running a business or corporation with financial, legal, accounting, and seasonal concerns that have to be deal with the minute someone becomes a business.

I have observed that the biggest time management issues for a small business owner are how to assign time to the tasks that will lead to the development of additional product (or customers or clients) versus keeping up with current or past customers or clients, and still finding the time to perform the tasks associated with running any business, such as invoicing, accounts receivable, inventory, "picking and packing," (if it is a business that involves shipping out goods), creating and maintaining a company web site, business correspondence, incoming telephone inquiries and calls, creating a catalog, handling returns, and on, and on, depending upon the specific type of business you are in.

Of course you could, and probably should, delegate some or all of the clerical tasks to a paid or unpaid (intern) assistant. You have to be careful, however, that you know enough about the way your business works – you have been in business long enough – that you are delegating tasks you have already mastered (so you will know if the person you're delegating to is doing it the right way or in the best interest of your company).

You may want to be in business at least six months to a year, doing almost everything yourself on purpose, before you begin to delegate certain business functions or job tasks. (This is a different approach to seeing the failure to delegate as a sign that you do not have the money to hire assistants.)

Many of the biggest companies started out with one or two persons doing everything out of their garage or the corner of their bedroom. It is only as the company grows to a certain size that administrative assistants, managers, or even outsourcing to mailing companies, begin to handle the time consuming, labor intensive aspects of the business that they had to do.

For Students

How many of the following questions can you answer "yes" to?

On a separate piece of paper, or photocopy this page, and answer the questions below with a *yes, sometimes*, or *no*.

1. I have a regular schedule for studying.
2. I have a specific place I always use to study.
3. I always get the course requirements before the semester begins so I can buy books ahead and plan.
4. My social life is planned around my exam schedule and required papers.
5. I start papers—planning/ researching—as soon as they are assigned.
6. I always have time to do extra readings in the areas I'm interested in.
7. I enjoy school and consider even tests or papers as challenging parts of the learning process.

Devise a plan to turn every *no* or *sometimes* into a *yes*. The information in this section should help you to accomplish that.

Let's look at the basics of time management in a school situation, remembering that the time pressures on someone returning to school later in life differ from those facing the younger student. Too, the student with a part-time or full-time job will conduct himself differently from one who doesn't work.

Each school year comes predefined as a block of time with certain objectives. Unlike a year-in, year-out, job, school is easily divisible into distinct periods with formal beginnings, well-defined endings, and structured checkpoints along the way. Take advantage of those clear divisions; it makes managing your time as a student somewhat easier.

Have an academic planning calendar that matches your schedule for the forthcoming year, and enter all course requirements (assignments, paper due dates, exams) that you know are due in the coming semester or school year onto your master calendar. Now, allocate certain blocks of time based on these commitments. For example, you might wish to reserve the week before midterms for studying so that you will not unnecessarily distract yourself week after final examinations for social and fun activities (and those inescapable duties you've put off while studying).

Some students find the "short shift" system of studying to be most effective. As one third-year law student put it: " I usually work in short shifts, of no longer than an hour, and I give myself incentives to push myself. Like I tell myself if I get through x a mount of work to do in the next hour, then I'll go play basketball for an hour." He's also a crammer, doing a lot of reading on his own, playing sports, and going out with his friends the rest of the time. " Right before finals, for a week or two, I do all the things I've been putting off all semester—most of my reading and studying."

A young woman, now 21, in her junior year of college in Oklahoma, and majoring in business administration, did not find cramming before exams worked for her. Her grades suffered so much because she went to football games rather than studying, that she dropped out of school for two years, and returned home to Florida to work for her father. Two years later, she returned to school, with a renewed commitment to apply herself.

Whether you study in short shifts or in long stretches, whether you study every night or cram right before exams, whether you retain what you learn only until the exam is over, or for the rest of your life, remembering and learning are the keys to success as a student—not how many hours you put in. In their book, *Study Smarts*, co-authors Kesselman-Turkel and Peterson, freelance writers and teachers, provide a summary of Dr. Walter Pauk's OK4R system, one of the many systems devised to help in remembering what you read. (OK4R is an acronym for *Overview, Key ideas, Read, Rite, Relate,* and *Review.)*

To save time learn speedreading and speedwriting.

You might find it helpful to have an orderly system for taking notes on what you're reading. The card that follows is a sample of one that could be adapted to your needs. (This particular one would be useful in doing a research paper, or familiarizing yourself with the literature on a given topic.)

Sample Bibliographic Information Entry

> Author(s):
> Title:
> Place of Publication:
> Publisher:
> Year of publication:
> Library Call # (if library book)
> Summary:
> Why This Work Is Important:
> Compared to Other Works:
> Criticism:
> Memorable quote(s) (include page # and quote):
> 1st reading:
> 2nd reading:

You will also need a place that is conducive to study—as quiet and free of distractions as possible. Some find library cubicles quiet; others can only study alone in an empty room. No one solution will work for everyone: a library may be best for some students, and a time waster for others (who can only study at the kitchen table).

Similarly, you might find, in spite of the costs involved, that purchasing books saves you time. Libraries are marvelous places to do research especially for older or out-of-print books, expensive references or directories, hard-to-find obscure works, and current or back issues of magazines and journals. For very new materials, however, especially paperback books, you may be better off acquiring these books because: (a) you want to own a copy for your professional or personal library; (b) it's so new the library is still awaiting the copies it ordered; (c) someone else has the book out on loan; and (d) you're too busy to get to the library.(Check if your library has a web site or will check availability of a title for you by phone.) However, don't fall into the trap of buying books, or photocopying articles or specific pages, that remain unread.

Now let's look at the time demands on the older student. Taking an occasional course in an adult education program, is one form of continuing or career education; it is relatively inexpensive and not very time-consuming. A commitment to a full-time degree program requires more of a juggling act—job, school, family, and friends—requiring sacrifices from everyone involved (but primarily from the student). At first, everyone may be sympathetic when studies preclude Thanksgiving this year at Cousin Rose's in Pennsylvania, but when you can't get away next year, or the following year, Cousin Rose may be distinctly less understanding.

Whether you are a typical young student or an older one, poor time management during the school term may contribute to test anxiety. A psychotherapist who runs workshops for overcoming test anxiety, says: "Not being adequately prepared, a cause of test anxiety, may be the consequence of procrastination about studying throughout the semester."

Behind procrastination and poor time habits can be fears of success and failure. Procrastination is an ineffective way of dealing with those conflicts.

Another time management consideration unique to students is that some, especially those who also work, may drive themselves at an inhuman pace for several years. Upon finishing school, it may be unrealistic and unhealthy to attempt to perpetuate those high-gear time schedules. Similarly, the other extreme—becoming lazy and without any drive as a reaction to those intense years—is just as ill-advised. Thus, while in the student role, if at all possible, pace yourself and include some socializing and relaxing as a training ground for creative time management in high-pressure situations.

For Teachers

Teachers traditionally are a very organized group. Indeed, the ability to organize a semester, a course, or a year-long plan of study often distinguishes the effective teachers from the breathless, anxious, and unprepared ones.

By having a firm grip on the overall demands for a specific course or class, you can then focus on how you deliver your material, as well as any extras. If you are uncertain about even what you need to present each day, or each week, it will be that much harder to enjoy your students or teaching.

Plan out the class or the year.

Aim for variety in your presentations, assignments, and materials.

Planning will enable you to see how often you are including audio-visual materials, straight lecture, discussion, or other varied techniques, such as role playing, acting out skits, using technology, and field trips.

Have a written record of each assignment as well as a summary of each day's lectures.

Make it clear what is required of your students in terms of classwork, homework, special reports or projects, tests, notetaking, and even opportunities for extra credit.

Build fun and surprises into your teaching.

Research finds that creative and learning are heightened by adding fun and interesting material to your teaching lessons.

Pace yourself.

Teaching can be even more intense over the 8 (for college) or 10 (for nursery through high school) months that you are working than it is for the typical office worker with just 2-3 weeks off a year. Pace yourself as much as possible throughout the year so that you are not so burned out by the end of May or the end of June, whenever the school year is over, that it takes you the entire summer vacation to recover (only to find, before you can even enjoy your time off, that you are right back at the beginning of another school year).

For the Job Seeker

A few years ago when Linda, a business statistics expert, thought she might lose her job because of cutbacks, she engaged in an organized job search. "I had an extensive plan," Linda explains. "I read books on career planning, such as Richard Bolles' *What Color*

Is Your Parachute?, how to write a resume, and how to find a job. I decided on the geographic area I would cover, and what type of job I wanted to explore. I actually made lists of people to contact in terms of networking and had four ways of searching my university alumni newsletter, newspaper advertisements, word-of-mouth, and meeting people who could give me general leads."

Fortunately Linda's search—which did lead to several firm job offers—became unnecessary once she learned she could keep her current job. That search, however, based on the fundamentals of time management, gave her confidence, and expertise, that she can apply if she ever wants to, or needs to, search again.

As Linda's successful job search demonstrates, an effective job search campaign is essentially a time management issue. In contrast to a haphazard approach, by applying the basics of time management—goal setting, planning, getting organized, prioritizing, to do lists, setting deadlines—your job search will be enhanced and facilitated. You will have immediate payoffs, in terms of finding a job, and long-term benefits, by developing an excellent reputation with potential employers for follow-up and efficiency.

As noted in the beginning of this book, there are two basic approaches to the way someone manages his or her time—reactive, whereby you respond to others' demands; and active, whereby you generate your own options. How you manage your time during your job search will be impacted by whether this is a reactive job search, because you have been fired, or have been told to find a new job; or an active one, in that you could stay at your current job, but you want to find another one. Linda's search was an active one.

By contrast, Bill, whose wife has a lucrative job that provides enough income for the two of them, is engaged in an unplanned reactive job search—if someone tells him of a potential job, he sends in a resume and hopes for the best. (After two years, he is still "looking"for a full-time job as a researcher.)

Whether or not you are currently employed will effect how you manage your time during this job search: if employed, you will have to find "hidden" time for your search before, during, or after work and personal obligations are fulfilled; if you are out of work, your biggest time problem may be to discipline yourself, somewhat like a freelance or self-employed professional or entrepreneur, to create a schedule, or structure, from which you will conduct your search.

You need to know where you are going so you know what to strive for and may plan how to get there. It is tempting to be concerned only with "the next job," but a professional five- or ten-year career plan will aid this and every job search. A broad goal, such as "I'd like to be a CEO" or "I'd like to earn over two hundred thousand a year," differs from a well-conceived plan. A plan includes what you want to be doing next year, and in five or ten years, as well as what jobs, or steps, you should take to achieve it.

Take a few minutes to ponder the following questions, writing down your considered answers:

In 15 years, I hope to be:
In 5 years, I hope to be:
In order to achieve those goals, my next job should be:

Now that you have a long-term career plan, and a "next step" short-term plan, you can zero in on your current job search, more confident that there is a focus and active component to your explorations. In this way, you will be less likely to just react to each and every job offer, no matter how at odds it is with your career plan.

Short-term planning will revolve around all the background research, phone calls, and interviews you will have to carry out in order to achieve your short-term goal, namely a new job. Once again, long-term plans aid short-term planning since you will be doing things, if you haven't been doing them all along that will make each search easier. You may decide, for example, that staying in touch with the key headhunters in your field is a time-saver even after you find a new position since your next search might be easier. You may also decide to continually update your resume, instead of reactively revising it because of a job crisis. Networking may become a long-term priority rather than just a short-term necessity.

Disorganization is an incredible time waster when searching for a new job. Develop a simple but effective information storage and retrieval system that works for you to easily keep track of phone numbers, correspondence, updated resumes and supporting materials, and research pertaining to this search, job hunting in general, as well as to specific companies.

Any number of filing systems could be effective for you: you could file alphabetically; have a "tickler file" by day or month; or file in categories. What's most important is not the kind of filing system you follow, but that you have one so you can quickly file, and retrieve, the information and materials that you need.

You may also have to go out "wide" with some job searches, meaning you will have to send a cover letter and resume to 50, 100, or even more potential employers. Especially when dealing in such numbers, time management skills are a definite plus.

A very effective time management tool when it comes to a job search is a written "to do" list. Like your filing system, "to do" lists may be constructed by any number of organizing principles, such as in order of importance (prioritizing), chronologically, or by linking similar tasks together. Whatever system you use, the vital point is to write it down, and do not cross an item off, or ignore it, until each item has been done, even if you carry that item on your revised "to do" list for days or weeks at a time. Learn to make estimates on how long a task will take you so you can get better at estimating when you could possibly finish each "to do" list item.

In addition to a to-do list, you should have a written or electronic planning calendar, preferably one you carry around with you, in which you enter right on the calendar, such as a daily diary large enough to hold this information, follow-up letters to write, or phone calls to initiate.

Remember that this job search may just be your number one priority. Until you achieve your goal of a new job, learn to say "no" to every optional request on your time that interferes. Furthermore, each job search will have priorities unique to that search so clarify what is most important to you, whether that includes rewriting your resume, taking a headhunter out to lunch, or going to a conference to learn about unadvertised job openings.

A key element to an effective job search campaign is follow-up. Follow-up includes everything from sending a thank you note to an interviewer or someone who recommended you for a job interview to following up on want ads, referrals, or requests for information by potential new employers. Definitely try to follow up on anything related to your specific job search immediately.

Balancing Work and Home Life

A magazine editor's husband stays at home and takes care of their two children while she's at the office. A woman with four children under the age of four, whose husband's salary is not enough, wants to take a job to earn some extra money and "just to get out of the house" a few hours a week. Two executives marry, have twins, and both continue working full time; they have fulltime help.

These are just a few examples of the multiplicity of situations, and choices, open to adults, single or coupled, with or without children. A woman's decision to work after marrying or becoming a parent is viewed today as a personal and economic decision; there are fewer rules than twenty-five years ago. Each woman, and couple, decides what's best; those decisions affect how they will spend their time. Time management will be affected by work arrangements, how many children are present, their ages, any available cleaning or child care help, and, in households of two or more, the division of labor agreed upon by the couple.

The theme that ran throughout my interviews with homemakers, whether or not they had other jobs, was that parenting obligations are their biggest time demand. (Those who stay home with young children, and do not work chose to be with their children and temporarily traded their own careers and additional income for full-time parenting responsibilities.) Few now look back on the nonparenting years as stressful in terms of time. Jessica, 32, a a full-time homemaker living in a Connecticut suburb, has two children, ages four and six, and is married to a lawyer. In comparing the years of her marriage before and after her children were born, Jessica says: "There was always time then. There's never enough time now." Marie, 31, a full-time homemaker in Queens, New York, is married to a schoolteacher and the mother of a two-year-old daughter. When her daughter was born, Marie quit her lucrative full-time job as production coordinator for a printer. "My husband and I refer to those early years of our marriage as the single years— married before kids," Marie says. Sara, 31, a corporate executive, married and the mother of a two-year-old, works full time, has full-time help at home, and prefers being at the office as much as any other nine-to-fiver. Sara says: "When I got married I told my husband, 'I don't like cleaning or cooking and I'm always going to work." And she has.

"I loved the job," Marie, who was earning over $40,000 a year, says, "but it was very high-powered and it became a bit much." For now, Marie wants to handle all the child-care responsibilities herself. Marie's cleaning chores are the same as before; she kept the cleaning lady that she used when she was working. Child-care demands structure her day but her husband, a school teacher, is home by three-thirty, so her days are short. The only chore Marie would like help with is cooking. "If tomorrow I wake up and I feel unhappy being home, I'll go back to work," Marie concludes, adding that I may have interviewed her on a "good day."

As noted in the next chapter, housekeeping chores are the least desirable aspect of homemaking reported by Oakley's study of London housewives. Hired help may not be feasible for economic reasons; even with help, there are still chores a homemaker may have to attend to. Jessica, the Connecticut housewife with two children, spends 5-1/2 hours each day doing household chores. Jessica explains: "Two hours for dinner. An hour a day for laundry. It takes me an hour to do [clean] the whole upstairs. Half an hour for breakfast and half an hour for lunch. Half an hour to pick them up at school. But I don't think of it that way because it's something I go along and do. And I don't keep a spotless house."

Parenting responsibilities, even if a parent works and has full-time help, usually consume the evenings and weekends. Jessica suggests spending as much time with your children as you enjoy, not more because you "should." "I like kids," Jessica says. "I can spend twenty-four hours a day, seven days a week with kids. Usually I need a break from kids once every three or four months. But it's important that if you don't want to spend a lot of time with your kids, you shouldn't do it, or feel guilty about [not doing] it. If you're happier working, you're going to have a much better relationship with your children, husband, friends [if you work]."

Corporations are recognizing that parenting presents time demands that may create stress for employees of either sex. In response to those pulls, companies are now sponsoring seminars during the workday to help employed parents cope better. A direct reaction to those seminars has been the formation of informal networks of parents within corporations who offer each other support about their mutual time problems.

Women who are full-time homemakers have time problems of a different sort from homemakers who also have outside jobs. Jessica explains: "Women who work don't have all the extracurricular things that the mothers who stay home have to do. They don't have to be the room mothers. They don't have to be the chauffeurs. They don't have to be the ones who get the calls when the kids in the neighborhood are sick. They don't have to allot time for certain things and they set their priorities differently."

Pam Young and Peggy Jones, sisters and mothers who were then fulltime homemakers, lifted themselves "out of the pigpen"— and wrote a bestseller about their program, *Sidetracked Home Executives*. They changed their lives by establishing and adhering to a time management system with just a few basic rules, such as: Wake up half an hour earlier than the rest of the family and get dressed; Make the bed before doing any other chores; Spend one weekday doing what you want to do (free of chores and errands).

"Time for myself" was a theme that homemakers with or without children, with or without outside jobs, stressed in our interviews. Whether it's working out at the gym, taking long walks alone, writing a novel while the baby is napping, or taking up yoga while the children are small, having personal and professional goals of one's own is important. Jessica explains: "I've always taken a day for myself. When my kids were little, one day a week I had a sitter. Now they're both in school so I don't find I [usually] need any more time than that. [But] if I need more time for myself, I'll get up at five in the morning, instead of seven, or I'll go to bed later."

An alternative to a full-time job for homemakers, especially those with small children, is part-time work inside or outside the home. Employment agencies have sprung up that cater to the part-time work needs of homemakers and potential employers.

Ironically, it is men, who are playing a more active parenting role, who are experiencing the family-work conflicts that women have always had. Don, 32, a research scientist, describes the impact his son's birth had on his work: "I found I wasn't going to the lab that much. When I did, I wasn't concentrating. I just wanted to be with my son. To watch him sleeping. To bathe him and feed him. I'm forcing myself to get back into my work now. I have to."

In the next chapter we will look at creative ways of improving your personal time management.

8
Improving Your Personal Time Management

Wherein lies happiness?
JOHN KEATS *(Endymion)*

The ones who find it hardest to improve their personal time are those who ask, "What free time? because they are unaware that most of their life is free time.

In a society that applauds accomplishment, doing something just for its own sake occupies a low priority. You don't run because you enjoy it, you do it to exercise the cardiovascular system. You don't join civic groups because you like to be around people, but to make contacts that will help your career. You don't sew because it's fun, but to save money. However, if you value yourself, and your own happiness, you'll want to make the most of your personal time. It is sad that for some, personal time—the time we truly do have more control over—can be less satisfying than the time spent working or doing the things that have to get done.

If you are prone to working too much, it may be as hard for you to make time for leisure activities as it is for someone with too little work incentive to work harder. If that's true, you might think of whatever you do outside of work as "productive leisure time" activities. James J. Sheeran in his book, *How to Skyrocket Your Income,* offers six productive leisure-time activities: 1) Become an expert (at something) ; 2) Try local politics; 3) Try teaching; 4) Become an omnivorous reader; 5) Increase communicative skills; and 6) Continue formal education.

Ask yourself this question: If I retired tomorrow, what would I want to do with my time? Whatever your answers are, pick one of those choices, and start doing it now.

Traveling is a leisure time activity that can occupy you (and your family) for months. You can read up on the possible places you want to visit, take time to contact friends to see if they know anyone who lives there, and explore ways to make the most of your stay.

One-day trips from your home—with or without a club—can provide memorable leisure-time fun. Weekend overnight trips, if you keep driving time to under two hours, may be time-saving mini-vacations.

Exercise

Exercising takes time. You've got to love it, relish the competition (if applicable), or believe it's so crucial to your health and well being that you'll make the time.

Consider several timesaving exercise suggestions:

1. Make exercise a part of your everyday routine—walk instead of taking the car, ride a bicycle on errands, do isometrics while you're on the phone, put in ten minutes of calisthenics every morning.
2. Keep your weight down so you exercise to stay fit, not principally as a weight-reducing measure.
3. If you absolutely hate exercising, try doing it with someone else, so it's a social as well as a physical activity; misery loves company.

4. Use the reward system discussed earlier "If I exercise this week, I'll . . ." At some point, you may find the exercising has become its own reward.

Decide now to create a regular and realistic exercise regimen, whether walking an extra two miles a day or taking a dance or karate class. Don't overload yourself by registering for nightly exercise classes. That kind of unrealistic over-commitment will probably result in abandoning the effort.

Make a commitment with yourself to begin a regular exercise/ sports regimen, alone, with your spouse, children, or a friend, even if it's only for 10 or 20 minutes every day, or three times a week. (Check with your physician before beginning any exercise program especially if you have been inactive for a long time, if you are overweight, or if you have any health problems that need to be addressed.)

Hobbies

A hobby can be a rewarding way to spend your time, especially since it can provide the "I did it all by myself" feeling.

If you don't have a hobby, think back to your early years. What did you like to do in your spare time then that you don't find time for now? Perhaps you watched the stars, burned designs in wood, or worked with mosaic tiles. Maybe you had a chemistry set or were an amateur photographer. No matter. You can learn a completely new hobby. The key is to become adept enough at your hobby so that it is something that gives you pleasure.

Hobbies are not, however, things you must do anyway. Try, if possible, to pick a hobby that is unrelated to your work. Example: You are a researcher and your profession requires you to read a lot. Reading could be your hobby, but only if you read something outside of your profession, such as short stories, mysteries, novels; poetry, or popular nonfiction.

Remember: you're not engaging in this hobby so you can

compete in a national contest or have a one-person showing of your work. Initially, and perhaps always, like exercise, this one's primarily for you.

Television

Watching television can be a worthwhile and inexpensive form of entertainment. In moderation, and if watched selectively, TV can be relaxing, informative, and stimulating. TV may also be a time-saver—you don't have to dress and travel to experience it. However, if it is your primary leisure-time activity, you will be missing out on a number of ways to creatively use your free time.

There always seem to be those who can do their homework, read a book, or prepare a report, all while watching television. If you are observant, you will find that either they are only watching television or only doing their homework. Their attention may shift back and forth but most of the time the television serves as background noise, or the book serves as facade for the television viewing.

How many hours do you spend watching TV, especially during the hours that are considered prime time (Monday through Saturday, 8:00 p.m. to 11:00 p.m. and Sunday, 7:00 p.m. to 11:00 p.m.)? Do you watch a specific program, or just whatever you happen to flip to? Do you even know your television viewing habits? Keep a TV log for the next week to find out the hours you watch, the programs you watch (and why), with whom you watch, and how much enjoyment you derive from your TV viewing.

Using a video cassette recorder (VCR) may help you diminish the total number of hours you spend watching TV. By fast forwarding through commercials, you can watch a two-hour movie in 90 minutes. A video cassette recorder enables you to tape a specific program and watch it when it is convenient for you. If you are away from home, for example, or doing something else, you need not stop to watch. In that way, your time is structured around your needs rather than the TV station's programming schedule. Add to this the fact that since you can freeze or stop the tape at any point, you can avoid inadvertently missing a major plot development because of other needs.

RELATIONSHIPS
Socializing/Entertaining

If possible, plan to see your friends, and to develop new acquaintances, around the times that are best for you. The holidays are a time for socializing and, generally, a favored time for entertaining—but if you happen to be studying for finals, or you're in a business with lots of year-end paperwork due right before or after the holidays, this may not be your best time.

Socializing, or getting together with friends or associates, takes place outside your home; entertaining is socializing inside your home—or in some other location you have chosen—for which you are responsible for supplying the food and drink or arranging for someone else to provide it.

To socialize, you might make a phone call or two, and decide when, where, and what (coffee at a cafe, movies, dinner, bowling, etc.), but there is very little "how" to be concerned about. The advance planning for socializing is minimal, yet, unless you have a drop-in arrangement with a friend who lives in the neighborhood or a coworker down the hall (potential time wasters, as we've seen), socializing takes some time and effort. Spur of the moment guests take the least amount of effort and preparation, especially if you've stockpiled suitable food and beverages. How often you socialize, and with whom, will depend on what value you place on that relationship as well as your other commitments.

What counts is not how busy you are, or how many people you see, but whether you feel that you are making enough time for socializing. You may find that there is sufficient socializing for you during the day or just after work that not socializing in the evenings and on the weekends is what you want. (You may be so over-socialized that you lack enough time for yourself or for your spouse.) You may want to schedule a night alone, or a night with your spouse, even if that means you simply read a book or watch

TV. Make sure you keep those appointments as surely as you would any other commitment.

Entertaining usually requires more advance planning. As veteran caterer and party-giver Florence Lowell points out in her book, *Be a Guest At Your Own Party*, entertaining is more fun when you're relaxed. Being relaxed, if you're the host or hostess, usually means planning ahead (even if that means merely picking a date, deciding whom to invite, and hiring someone to carry out your plans for you.)

You can make such a big deal about entertaining that you never find the time. If, you usually keep your home reasonably clean, you won't associate entertaining with "cleaning up." The more frequently you entertain, the more comfortable you'll become at doing it. When it comes to entertaining, however, Murphy's Law is in effect more than ever—it almost always takes more time, energy, and money than you thought it would. Keeping this in mind, the simpler you make your entertaining, the more likely you will be to do it again. However, you have to be careful not to offend your guests; if they believe there was no effort involved, they may feel that you don't think they matter very much.

Make a list of your closest friends and relatives. Make a second list of those business associates and casual friends or acquaintances that you'd like to invite over. Now look ahead at the coming year. How frequently do you want to entertain? Are there times that are better for you (or your family) than others?

Look over your list of names. Figure out what forms your entertaining should take to include these varying individuals and groups. You might, for example, have a small birthday party for your father-in-law, or a huge bash for your whole office. Have one friend over for coffee and cake, perhaps in two months, and invite two couples for dinner, three months from now. If one of your goals is to enable all your guests to have a chance to interact with one another, consider entertaining up to eight persons at the same time. Larger groups will result in some of your guests leaving as unfamiliar to others as when they arrived (which is just fine in a large party situation.)

Have you ever considered giving two parties back-to-back? Those you couldn't include in the first party can be served at the second, and since your hall closet is already cleaned out, why not save time and get extra mileage out of your efforts? Have you also considered serving brunch, in lieu of dinner? It usually takes less time to plan, prepare, serve, and clean up.

Friendships

Make time for your friends. Friendships need time to develop and to be maintained. Certainly not as much time as you invest in a spouse, child, or parent, but if you let other commitments come between you and a close or best friend, you may find your friend has replaced you with someone more available. A worthwhile friend is worth that time. (For a detailed exploration of friendship, see J. Yager, *Friendshifts®: The Power of Friendship and How It Shapes Our Lives.)*

Friendship provides benefits that may be lacking in a family. As one 37-year-old single woman told me: "Your family accepts you with all your faults and they love you anyway, but it's not like that with your friends." She was alluding to the fact that your friends choose you. To reinforce their choice of you (and your choice of them) you will need time together, as well as the ability to be open up (self-disclosure), trust each other, and to be vulnerable (able to withstand the possible end of the friendship).

Here are some suggestions for finding time to get together with your friends no matter how busy you are:

- Call each other just to say hello and chat, not just to share the "big" good or bad news.
- Return phone messages promptly; if you cannot, let your friend know why – e.g. you will be away. But grant your friend some slack if he or she does not return your call right away since there might be a reason (being out of town, phone machine failed, a child failed to deliver the message, etc.)
- Make a commitment to get together on a regular basis, depending upon time and distance, on your own or with your spouses or families.
- Plan vacation time together.

- Keep postcards with you so if you have a spare moment while waiting in the doctor's office, sitting around while your child is taking guitar lessons or playing soccer, or while you're on a business trip, you can write to your friends.
- Remember your friends' birthdays by calling, sending a card, or getting together. Birthday presents don't have to cost a lot or could even be something homemade.
- When you do speak or get together, plan another time for your next reunion.
- If your friend is going through changes or has something new demanding more of her or his time, cut her or him some slack if she's or he's not returning phone calls as quickly or at all, and don't stand on ceremony. Call her or him.
- Make a commitment to be there for each other –physically as well in spirit — for all major events in your lives if it is at all possible.
- If you have a conflict, deal with it, or let some time pass till you are able to work things through with your friend to get your relationship back on track.
- Think before you speak.
- Respect your friend's boundaries. Certain topics may be off-limits, such as spouses or childrearing issues, even if gossiping about dates when you were single together was completely acceptable.
- *Celebrate* your friend's triumphs. Though competitive feelings are normal, deal with yours so it does not sabotage your friendship.
- On occasion or regularly, have a "Friends Night Out."
- Volunteer together.

Making Time for Partners and Children

Ironically it can be easier to find time for friends than for mates and children. In an intimate setting, physical presence need not mean that you're giving time. (You could be going your separate ways even under the same roof.) Friendship, since you're generally separated, requires time and effort if contact is to be maintained, whether by phone, letter, or in person. It is usually necessary to make an appointment for meeting, even if it only means calling a few minutes in advance to say, "Can I come over?" Because contact is generally less frequent than with family members, and because the relationship is less intimate, different rules apply.

Friends may even give each other more attention when they do get together than family members regularly get because the family is around all the time. Furthermore, your expectations are lower from a friendship than from a primary intimate relationship. It may be enough for friends to get together once a month to play tennis; few marriages would tolerate that dearth of interaction.

Time for Partners

If you feel you don't have enough time with your spouse, perhaps some of the following suggestions will be useful:

- Realize that perfect relationships exist only between perfect people.
- If possible, spend some time together during the workday, perhaps meeting for lunch on occasion, so you're not just an "after five" couple.
- Don't wait for your annual vacation to get away, plan mini-getaway weekends together to break up your routine.
- If you feel a need to get away alone now and then, do it. It doesn't necessarily mean there's something wrong with your relationship; a little absence does make the heart grow fonder.
- How much do you really know about what your partner does? Take the time to read books, take courses, and talk to others in that line of work (and vice versa) so you can better understand each other's daily experiences.
- Have a leisure activity that you regularly do together.
- Share parenting and household responsibilities by working them out in a way that's best for both of you.
- Especially when your children are younger, get out at least once a week as a couple. Hire a babysitter, ask a trusted relative to help out sitting, or work out an exchange system with a neighbor or friend you have confidence in: you watch my child and I'll watch yours.

What about sexual intimacy? Once again, personal preferences as to frequency, duration, style, and enjoyment are paramount, but if sex is important to you and your partner, make the time for it, no matter how busy you are. Although sexual intimacy is associated with marital bliss, some, such as Herbert G. Zerof in *Finding Intimacy*, say it is being overemphasized today.

If you are giving sex the proper emphasis in your relationship, however, but are failing to find time for it, sex therapist Avodah Offit, in *Night Thoughts*, suggests making the time. Offit advises couples, on a regular basis, to set aside time exclusively devoted to their intimate relationship. If you wait to be spontaneous, it may never happen.

No time at night? Set your alarm an extra half an hour or hour earlier. Other suggestions? Bring your children to the babysitter or relative and spend a few hours at home, alone for a change, or treat yourselves to a few hours at a nearby hotel. You may be able to negotiate a lower rate if you just want the room for a few hours rather than staying overnight. If you feel comfortable leaving your children with a trusted sitter or relatives, consider going away together for a day or two or even a week. If you or your spouse has to go on a business trip, if appropriate, you might consider accompanying him or her.

Time for Children

Consider the quality, and quantity, of time you spend with your children. How much time do you give to them? "It's important to spend time with your children because they need to know they're loved and cared about," says Linda, 31, a full-time college student who is also the mother of three children, ages 13, 11, and 4. "If you don't spend time with them, they won't feel that they're wanted, loved, or needed. They have to be taught. It takes time to teach them the proper things—values, morals, and all those things," Linda adds.

Here are some tips for finding the time for your children, even as they get into the teen years:
- Commit to a nightly family dinner or at least having meals together on the weekends.
- Spend at least some time over the weekend doing a "family

activity," e.g. going to the movies, bike riding, bowling, skating, and doing volunteer work together.

• Have one night a week that is family game night. At every age level, you can play store-bought games as well as original ones.

• No matter how busy you are at work, find a way to take at least a week each year for a family vacation. Even if you lack the funds to go to Europe or a faraway expensive vacation, plan trips and activities to do together as a family.

• Establish traditions that promote making time for each other, such as baking together for holidays, designing and sending out greeting cards together, and celebrating the traditional family-related holidays, such as Mother's Day or Father's Day, together.

Time For Yourself

We all need some time alone in addition to time with others. If one partner is around people all day, and the other is not, he or she may have opposite needs during non-work time. Similarly, children may want their parents' attention and the parent may not have any attention to give just then.

Management consultant Gisele Richardson has noted that people need three types of time for emotional health: diffused time (exposure to people); qualitative time (one-on-one intimate contact); and alone time (private moments to digest the stimuli from the other two types of time.)

If someone needs "alone time" it shouldn't be taken as rejection. You, or others, should use the time that would have been spent with others to your best advantage; you will all appreciate the time together even more when you do have some.

TIME MANAGEMENT AT HOME

Here are some time-effective strategies for necessary chores—food shopping, cleaning, washing clothes, vacuuming—tasks that almost everyone faces. Unless you are that very rare individual who loves housework, doing these jobs faster will be a welcome time saver. Not surprisingly, Ann Oakley, who studied how London housewives behave, reported in *The Sociology of Housework* that housework was the aspect of married life that the women she interviewed liked least. For the 40 women closely studied by Oakley, the housewives had an average workweek of 77 hours (versus the average 40-hour worker's week). As the number of children increased, so did the number of hours at their job. Interestingly, the one woman in her sample with a full-time job outside the home spent only 48 hours doing house-related work. Perhaps housework (including shopping and childrearing activities), like other tasks, will expand to fill the number of available hours—unless you have a plan.

With so many women working and unavailable for fulltime housekeeping chores, including married women with young children, finding ways to speed up household chores is a necessity. Men are pitching in—to be sure, some more than others are—and they also need ways to get the job done as quickly, and as pleasantly, as possible. If you live alone, housekeeping chores are all yours; you'll probably want to do them quickly so you have more time for other things.

The perfectionist may spend waking hours cleaning, puttering, and worrying about every minor detail in the home. Unless you are willing to devote that kind of full-time attention to your home, you might consider modifying your standards of cleanliness and orderliness. If you have been knocking yourself out dusting every other day, you might try doing it once a week and see if it makes a difference to anyone (including you).

Fear of failure or success may also be a factor in taking too long with housework. If a woman is afraid of competing in the job world (and sees it as a man's world), she may stretch out the time housekeeping takes to justify her not getting a job. She may fear competing at an outside job and use housework to keep busy so she doesn't run the risk of any actual or fantasized repercussions.

The inability to say *no* could be another time waster behind inefficient household maintenance. Especially as children mature, housework should be delegated to each person, not just to the mother, or father, who cannot say "no" when asked to do this or that chore.

Housework also provides instant gratification: results of your efforts are clearly visible when a sink full of dishes disappears or a room is transformed by your purchases. Success in a career may not be so readily apparent. At work, responsibilities may be vague; at home, not only are the responsibilities ongoing and consistent—beds always need to be made, towels need to be washed again—but once a homemaker sets up a ritual, all that's required is steady labor.

There is no single time-effective way to do household chores. Some find a fixed schedule best; others prefer to work *ad hoc*. One retired man jogs after he prepares the salad he's made and put in the refrigerator for dinner. By the time he returns, his wife is back from her full-time job, and dinner's ready. What matters is having a system that works for you so that household chores do not consume time that could be spent in a more meaningful way.

BECOMING ORGANIZED AT HOME

Obviously it is easier to organize an apartment or a home if you have just moved in. Everything is still in boxes, you put up those extra shelves in the pantry, you decide what will go where in each of the closets, you categorize your books as you put them back on the shelves, and so forth. Most of us are already living somewhere, however, and we would like to reorganize our living space without having to move out.

You will save time, and enjoy an uncluttered and pleasant environment, if you start organizing your home, one room or one project at a time. Divide your home up in a way that will make organizing or reorganizing it easiest for you. The most obvious ways of approaching this would be—

     By project (e.g., closets, drawers, shelves, etc.)
     By room (e.g., living room, dining room, kitchen, etc.)

Consider starting from your front door and working your way

through your apartment or home. First, concentrate on what shows as soon as you enter your home. Seeing the results of organizing your living room or guest bathroom will reaffirm your efforts.

Investing time in creating order will save you countless hours of time for a long time to come.

Second, tackle the more challenging "hidden" areas of disorder, like inside the closets and drawers. Only you, and those with whom you live, will benefit from these organizational efforts. The payoff will be even greater than the compliments received from guests who are impressed by your neat living room.

Systematically organizing your home a room, or an area, at a time may work best for you. That approach allows you to fully explore all the needs that you or your family want that area or room to fulfill. Example: Is your living room where you want to have a study corner for handling paperwork or is it just a place to entertain? Your answer to that question will help you to reorganize your space accordingly. Your dresser drawers can have dividers, so that socks, shirts, undergarments, underwear, and other everyday pieces of clothing are easily organized (and located). For women, a lingerie chest, with small, multiple drawers, is a useful way to organize such small items as pocketbooks, gloves, summer tops, and scarves, in addition to lingerie and undergarments.

Consider organizing the kitchen. You want to have most accessible to you those materials that you need and use most frequently. (This is based on the same Active and Inactive organizing principle that you have applied to your files.) Keep in another part of the kitchen, or even in another room, those materials that you do not use regularly. You may decide your kitchen needs a waste can at both ends, to cut down on unnecessary walking.

Proximity, especially in the kitchen, will save you minutes each day, and hours each week in food preparation, serving, clean up, and in general household maintenance.

It is useful in organizing each area in your home to think of each part of the whole as important in and of itself. For example, the way you organize inside the refrigerator and inside the freezer can save you as much time as how you organize your cabinets and drawers. A well-organized closet or garage can also save you and your family member from hours searching for gloves or a helmet.

Keep in mind all the organizing principles that you learned in Chapter 5 including the following timesaving guidelines:

Frequently used items should be kept in accessible places.
Have a specific place for everything.
Any removed item must be returned to its designated place.
Eliminate clutter.
Periodically go through all your possessions and give away, throw out, or rearrange to suit your current needs.
Create and follow to-do lists for your home-related obligations.
Delegate whenever possible.

Household Responsibilities

Even if you hire someone to organize your home, you will probably have to do the day-to-day maintenance. Everyday maintenance, however, like making the beds or preparing and serving dinner, is often easier to find time for than seasonal timely chores like cleaning the windows, washing the car, or planting the flowers and vegetables. Whether you live alone, with a roommate, or with children, consider delegating specific tasks to others. If those you live with will not, or cannot, do these chores, you might, if you can afford it, consider delegating some of them to paid workers, e.g., window washers, cleaning ladies, someone to do the laundry. If you cannot afford to pay someone for doing those heavy household tasks, consider what skills you can offer or barter in exchange for someone else doing the housework you despise.

If you have a roommate of the same sex, dividing up the household chores may be easier than if you are married. (Socialized expectations about the wife's role in housekeeping complicate what a woman or a man " should" do even if both are working full-time.) For same-sex roommates, make a list of housekeeping tasks and simply decide whose job it is— permanently or an alternating basis.

If you are a parent, have you considered what responsibilities your child can handle even at a very young age. In addition to "feeding my doll, playing with my sister, and being a good girl," a four-year-old girl in Massachusetts gave a list of household responsibilities that are hers alone or that she helps with:

clean up my toys
dress myself
feed the fish
rake the leaves
wash the car
make my bed
wash up
let Daddy sleep late on Sunday

Giving children household responsibilities, and increasing those responsibilities as they grow, takes up less of your time than trying to do it all and complaining about your martyrdom.

HOUSEHOLD PROJECTS

Whether you are decorating an apartment or home for the first time, or renovating one or more rooms where you've been living for a while, *decorate for efficiency as well as comfort and appearance.* It's best to take things one step at a time. In a new home, you can do one project at a time (refinishing all the floors, painting, building wall units, for example); if you're renovating, you may more readily do it a room at a time. In both situations, follow the same time management rules that you've been learning: *Set your priorities and then, in an orderly fashion, go about carrying them out.*

How do you proceed? Do you hire a decorator? Do you try to do it yourself? Hiring a decorator may save you time, but it will be more expensive. You may also lose the creative pleasure of carrying your own ideas through to completion. If you select, trust, and hire a decorator, he can supervise the changes, while you do something else. Hiring a decorator is not simply a matter of finding a name in the telephone directory. You'll need to visit homes he's decorated to see if his concepts and yours are compatible; you'll need to talk with him; you'll need to provide ideas, consider his suggestions, and approve a proposed budget and the completed work. You certainly don't want to hand a check to a decorator and thereafter live in his or her concept of "home."

If major purchases are involved, you should have any necessary structural changes (putting up or tearing down walls/ windows/doors, sanding and staining floors, painting, scraping old wallpaper and repapering) completed before the new or recovered furniture arrives. Any processes involving caustic chemicals, paints, sanding, or dust can damage furniture, rugs, and even houseplants.

It may be cost-ineffective to do major work yourself, including repairs. Unless you are a professional and know what you're doing, these are complex tasks, both to learn and to carry out properly. In addition, you will have to rent or purchase all the equipment necessary to complete the job. Finally, if you botch the job, you will have to pay for professionals to undo your mess, and then redo things correctly.

HOUSEHOLD MAINTENANCE
Cleaning, Laundry, and Errands

The best overall time saver in your home or apartment is this: *Make it maintenance-free.* Invest the extra time and money to eliminate as many ongoing cleaning demands as you can: tweed rugs camouflage dirt better than solid ones; high-gloss enamel paint in the kitchen or children's rooms easily wipes clean; durable furniture does not readily show or accept stains, and needs only occasional vacuuming; plastic tablecloths are easier to care for than cloth ones; carefully planned storage units ensure that everything has a place, and tidying up is minimized.

In *Is There Life After Housework?* Don Aslett, president of a cleaning business that he founded, gives this advice about making your home or apartment as maintenance-free as possible: "Work can be lessened, and time saved, by good maintenance planning and decorating.... A bathroom is no place for elaborate bookcases, statues, or other unmaintainable furniture and fixtures. Keep in mind the following: 1. Will it clean? 2. Will it last? 3. Is it usable?"

Create a housekeeping time log or inventory, and base it on the time you *think you* spend in performing each of the major household chores. Then, time yourself and write down the *actual* time spent. You won't feel "on top of things" unless you know how much time you really need/spend, and can allot that much, with a little extra for the "anything that can go wrong" syndrome.

Another way to save lots of time is to purchase six months' worth of household items—especially toiletries and nonperishable maintenance supplies—and have them on hand. Shopping in quantity, and in advance, also allows you to get the best prices. For storage, use the active/inactive principle: most frequently used items most accessible, backup items nearby and surplus items still available but not "at hand."

Another time saver is to compile an up-to-date list of those services and professionals that you may need in the course of maintaining a residence.

Some find it faster to do their household chores before leaving for their office; it sets a time limit on a limitless task and also enables them to look forward to chore-less evenings and weekends. Forty-year-old Gloria, uses Saturdays from 9 a.m. to 2 p.m. to do the week's cleaning. Carol, whose four children are grown and on their own, does her cleaning in the evenings, from 9 p.m. to 11 p.m., after she has prepared, served, and cleaned up dinner. She prefers to do cleaning on weekday nights, since she works full-time, so the weekends, her husband's and her only time to socialize, are clear. For many families, Saturday morning is "cleaning day," with everyone pitching in.

Make sure that the appliances you use for cleaning are the best you can afford.

To save time on errands, make use of as many pick-up and

delivery services as you can. If you have to do it in person, try to do several chores at the same time—leaving some days completely errand-free. For example, pick up your shoes, dry cleaning, and the newspaper in just one trip.

Laundry should not be the time-consuming task that some make it out to be. Do multiple loads daily, or every other day, depending upon volume, if you have enough reserve items. At a laundromat, it takes about the same time (if sufficient machines are available) to do five loads as to do two. If you have a machine in your home, let the machine run while you do other things. Clock exactly how long the washing machine and/or dryer take so you can use that time productively doing something else. You might also consider using a laundromat that will do the work for you.

Household Directories/Records

It will save lots of time in the long run if you have an effective record-keeping system, whether for household financial matters (income, expenses, tax deductions, contributions, etc.) or for health matters (names of physicians and past medical problems, name of any medication currently being taken, dates of vaccinations, etc.).

An important consideration is: Enter the information as soon as it is available or it will not be readily available when needed. To keep track of expenses, consider a pocket-sized expense record that you can carry around with you, right in your wallet or pocketbook, so that you can enter information as you go along.

One way to keep track of physician visits is to schedule all semi-annual and annual check-ups during the same two-week period each year, or on or around a memorable date, such as your child's birthday, for his or her annual check-up. Then, when that time of year comes around, it's a reminder that it's time to go for your check-ups.

Create a list of personal records (credit card numbers, driver's license number, etc.), and keep it in a safe place (not your wallet)! Also create a list of key names and phone numbers that is kept up to date to facilitate contacting any of these services or professionals quickly, such as fire and police department, and physicians.

Food: Preparation, Shopping, Storage, and Cleanup

Food is one of the necessities in life and, if you are not organized about it, one of the biggest time-drainers—even several hours a day. If you have been solely responsible for all the meals, you might consider weaning your family away from this dependency with one or both of the following ideas: have a "fend for yourself night," or ask your spouse if just one night a week, dinner could be his or her responsibility.

You might also consider doing all your cooking for the weekend on Fridays—preparing tuna fish, egg salad, shrimp salad, and pot roast, for example—so that you can have a completely non-cooking weekend. If you've been cooking every night, you might try ordering in or eating out once a week, if the budget can bear it. Remember, eating out may not save time—you've got to get to the restaurant, order, eat, and get back—but at least you don't have to think about what you'll prepare, or do the cooking, serving, and cleaning up afterwards.

Saving time in the kitchen requires planning—you need a clear idea of what you're going to do, and what equipment or ingredients you need, as well as directions for carrying out your plan. One married woman of 65 (who worked full-time even while her three children were small) never starts a dish until all the ingredients are on hand and in front of her on the kitchen counter.

Follow the suggestions at the beginning of this chapter for organizing your kitchen. You might also consider having close at hand a chart listing the use for each spice and condiment.

The microwave has revolutionized mealtime preparation; it is now considered an indispensable, time-saving piece of kitchen equipment even if a conventional oven seems favored for preparing some dishes from scratch (or reheating certain foods).

Food processors may save you time mixing dough or grinding large quantities of food. For chopping vegetables, however, the consensus seems to be that a sharp knife and your hands are the fastest method. By contrast, electric mixers and juicers are faster than comparable equipment relying on arm power.

When shopping and storing food, find out, and keep in mind, the storage capacity and shelf life of specific perishables, frozen and canned foods. Consider stocking dehydrated and freeze-dried foods, which will usually last even longer than canned goods. You should also check your pantry, from time to time, making sure you are not keeping (and opening yourself up to the possibility of using) canned or dry goods past their stamped expiration date.

To save time food shopping, keep a pad and pencil in your kitchen to jot down items as you realize you need them. You might also create a master grocery list, and have blank forms on hand, bringing a completed form with you on your trip to the supermarket.

. Make a plan—decide on a menu, whether for breakfast, lunch, or dinner—and execute your plan as quickly as possible. The biggest time waster in the kitchen is to select ingredients willy-nilly and try to pull a meal together. Unless you're a "born" cook, try to have at least ten or twenty recipes memorized or nearby that you and your family enjoy. For those nights you just don't want to take the time to cook, ask your partner or, if they are old enough, your children to prepare the meal. Also have a list of restaurants or food services handy that you can call to order in dinner. If it doesn't offend your environmental sympathies, have paper plates and cups on hand for those times when you don't want to take the time to do the dishes.

In the next and last chapter you will find 125 top time-saving ideas in these key areas: the top ten creative time management ideas; basic principles, goal-setting, organizing, overcoming obstacles to time management (time wasters), equipment and technology, work time, delegating, shopping, office or household maintenance, holiday time, and personal time.

9
125 TOP
TIME-SAVING IDEAS

Pythagoras, when he was asked what time was, answered that it was the soul of this world.

PLUTARCH (*Platonic Questions*)

You now know basic guidelines for creative and effective time management at work and in your leisure hours. Here to reinforce the key concepts and to share some new ideas are 125 useful time-saving ideas.

The top ten time-saving ideas

1. *Practice the 7 principles of creative time management:*
1. Be active, not reactive; 2. Set short and long-term goals;
3. Prioritize actions; 4. Keep your focus; 5. Create realistic deadlines; 6. D-O I-T N-O-W; and 7. Balance your life.

2. *D-O I-T N-O-W*

D – Divide and conquer what you have to do.

O – Organize your materials, how you will do it.

I – Ignore interruptions that are annoying distractions.

T – Take the time to learn how to do things yourself.

N – Now, not tomorrow.

O – Opportunity is knocking.

W– Watch out for how much time is being spent on the Internet, watching TV, or talking on the phone.

3. *Be focused yet flexible.* Don't spread yourself too thin. Do one thing at a time but know when doing two things at once, like listening to a book on tape (audiobook) while commuting, is okay. Be flexible and open to revising your goals or activities based on new information.

4. *Rejoice in your fans and in your mentors.* Seek out, invest time in, and give sincere thanks to those who celebrate and help *you*--your values, your capabilities, your work, your relationships.

5. *Become a creative time manager.* Take the time to master effective time management. The skills will take you far and help you feel less stressed and able to lead a more balanced life.

6. *Keep physically fit.* Being out of shape, or in ill health, makes you less efficient.

7. *Use the ABC approach.* A. Knowing what you've got. B. Knowing what you want. C. Using A and B to get what you want by asking "who, what, where, when, why, and how".

8. *Use the verb-noun principle.* Simplify your goals and determine your short- and long-term priorities by dividing your goal into a noun and a verb. Just two words. "Finish book." "Write report." "Call hotel." "Learn software." "Hire publicist."

9. *Listen to your inner voice about how to spend your time right now.* What would you want to do with your time if you found out you had just two months to live? Unless you would say, "exactly what I'm now doing," why not do *now* whatever you've put off?

10. *Empower yourself.* Of course chance and fate are factors, but focus on how much control you *do* have. Remember *you* are the master of your life—and your time.

Basic principles

11. Concentrate. Eliminate self-made interruptions and distractions. Minimize interruptions imposed on you by others, especially automatically talking whenever you get a phone call

even if it is an inconvenient time for you.

12. Categorize your work, school, household, and personal responsibilities; focus on doing what you have to, and want to do, one task at a time.

13. Break down major tasks into small ones so: a) the work is more manageable; b) you can reward yourself for completing each step; c) you can keep better track of your progress; d) you will reduce the tendency to do too much at once; and e) you can set more realistic deadlines to complete each small step.

14. Be careful about basing decisions on the wrong information or on forming alliances with saboteurs in business or in your personal life, potential causes of mismanaged time.

15. Find your "hidden" time, and guard it carefully, such as going to bed an hour later, getting to work an hour earlier, waking up two hours earlier, or more productively using commuting time.

16. Don't worry and fret about the future or feel guilty about the past. Be aware of how the past teaches you, and how your current plans and efforts can improve the future.

17. If you don't know, find out, or ask someone who does whose opinion and knowledge you respect and trust.

18. Use your judgment and follow up as needed– on phone calls, on inquiries, on whether or not a fax was successfully received, on submissions.

19. Deal with crises immediately, before they become overwhelming obstacles to your goals.

20. Figure out the best way to handle each situation—by phone, by mail, by E-mail, or in person.

21. If there are major changes coming up in your life, adjust your time budget to accommodate them.

22. Group and complete similar tasks together.

23. Promise less, deliver lots more.

24. If possible, return phone calls the same day.

25. Do what you have to do first, not what is easiest.

26. Find out what others want you to do. Make sure, as long as you agree with their demands, that you first give them what they ask for, and then do anything extra.

27. Watch out for the "little" things that may have a tendency to fall through the cracks or, if ignored, may become "big" things.

28. There is a place within each of us where creative and innovative work is nurtured and developed. It is usually necessary to have inner calm, not chaos, for optimum thinking, efficiency, and to maximize your ability to concentrate.

29. Effective time managers make everyone, and everything, seem as if she or he (or it) is her or his only concern at that moment.

30. Be prepared ahead so when the time comes to do something it doesn't take you longer than necessary.

31. Read instructions carefully to avoid wasting everyone's time including your own.

32. Of course you should wear a watch, or be near a clock that is visible to you, but make sure whatever time piece you are depending on is accurate and reliable down to the exact minute. Put a clock in every room, including the bathroom.

33. You often do not know what is going on in someone else's life so be patient until you find out why a call is not returned, a fax, letter, or E-mail is not answered. Be patient and let them contact you. If you must get an immediate answer, *graciously* follow-up.

34. It takes the same amount of time to be pleasant to others as to be nasty, but pleasant and nice will get you much further.

35. A little pressure is a motivator; too much pressure usually shuts people down so be realistic about what you can and cannot accomplish, and set realistic deadlines.

36. Know yourself – your strengths, your weaknesses, what works best for you, and take what is special about you into account in your business and personal activities.

37. Become attuned to your body's energy highs and lows. When are you most alert? tired? able to concentrate? Try to plan your daily and evening activities around your natural body rhythm.

38. If you know what you should be doing (but you're not doing it, for whatever reason), you're a lot better off than most, who are in such a fog they do not even know that they don't know what they should do or how they might best spend their time *now*.

39. The more you do, the more you *can* do.

40. Sometimes you have to slow down, at least temporarily, in order to go faster in the long run. Learn to recognize when it is time for such a deliberate respite.

41. Learn speedreading as well as how to read material quickly, especially business writing and nonfiction, highlighting key points.

Goal setting

42. Figure out what will make the difference in your career, or in your personal life, and do that FIRST. Focus your energies on that specific project or relationship. Only go on to your next goal, or project, when you have completed the PRIORITY task at hand.

43. Write down your short (daily) and longer-term goals.

44. Focus, focus, focus.

45. Create a professional and a personal or family mission statement. What do you really value? Write down your mission statement. Date it. Review and revise it periodically.

46. Having enough time is both a reality, and a subjective perception. If you are unrealistic about how much you can accomplish in any given period of time, you will always feel as if you are "out of time." Set realistic and attainable goals.

47. Use special days, such as your birthday, New Year's Day, or your work starting date anniversary to reassess how you are handling your goals. Date each assessment and keep it stored in your "Everything Notebook," planning calendar, diary, or journal.

48. Don't waste time reinventing the wheel. Learn from the examples of others and then make your goals to do it better, faster, or in a different way than anyone else.

49. Create a business plan for your job, business, or career. Refer back to it on a regular basis to assess your progress.

Organizing

50. Develop a system for tracking your daily activities, such as a "things to do" list.

51. Eliminate clutter. Allot time for periodic sifting and sorting: discard, give away, or sell surplus possessions.

52. Organize your office and home so everything is accessible;

use *active* and *inactive* criteria for placing items.

53. Use an organizing principle for organizing your files: alphabetically, by number, color, chronologically, etc.

54. For a few, a messy desk is the sign of genius. For most, a messy desk is a sign of disorganization and neglected paperwork. Budget regular time to file and clear off your desk.

55. Get into the habit of dating what you are working on so it will be easier to keep it organized. Date written material on the front or back; incorporate a date into the name of a computer file.

56. To avoid lateness, give yourself an extra 10 or 15 minutes to get to appointments.

57. If you need additional help organizing and getting rid of clutter, take a course or a seminar, hire a time management consultant, read articles or books, or watch a related video.

58. Use the annual Getting Organized Week, sponsored by NAPO (National Association of Professional Organizers), the first week of October each year, as a target date.

59. Create your own days or dates, on a weekly, monthly, or annual basis, to clean off your desk, out your files, your closets, or to overhaul your organizing system.

60. Have handy the names, addresses, phone numbers, and, pick up schedule for charities, recycling, or resale shops that will welcome your old stuff or reading materials to get rid of your clutter.

Overcoming time management obstacles (time wasters)

61. If you have a tendency to do too many things at once, wait till you finish something before tackling the next project.

62. Learn to say "no" easily, politely, and without guilt.

63. If you have a tendency to procrastinate, make sure you give yourself a deadline with "mini-deadlines" along the way.

64. Sometimes delay is good (and not procrastinating) such as waiting to reread something before submitting it. But if you are really procrastinating, don't feel guilty about it, which will probably lead to more procrastinating.

65. Make whatever you are procrastinating about the first thing you do in the morning. Do not go on to anything else until you

have that priority task completed.

66. If you are a perfectionist, shift your drive from unattainable perfection to striving for excellence, a more realistic goal.

67. If you have a problem with lateness, time exactly how long each task (dressing, commuting, etc.) takes you; make an appointment with yourself to leave at a certain time so you will be on time.

68. If you stay on the phone too long, keep a clock or egg timer near your phone. Notice how much time is passing and learn to handle phone conversations in a more succinct way.

69. If you're always running late in the morning, do everything sooner — wake up earlier, eat breakfast earlier, and leave your house or apartment earlier.

70. Remember, in terms of lateness, that there are, however, cultural differences. As French and Spanish businesspeople noted, fifteen minutes late in their countries is not considered "late" the way it would be in the United States.

71. Find out as far in advance as possible what family responsibilities you have to deal with so you can budget work or personal time for those commitments.

72. Plan for better use of commuting or business travel time. Keep handy in your car or attache case, tapes, reading and writing material, a computer, or a portable tape recorder.

73. If fear of failure is holding you back, put your energy into doing more preparation and training to build up your confidence (which will help overcome a failure fear.)

74. See criticism as feedback, rather than criticism. If the feedback is valuable, use it. If not, ignore it.

75. It's unproductive to defend yourself if you were in the wrong. If appropriate, apologize, learn from your mistake, and move on without ruminating over the situation.

76. Boredom may be a signal that there are certain tasks you should be delegating.

77. Learn what obstacles to effective time management (time wasters) slow you down, such as complaining or perfectionism, and work on overcoming each and every one.

Equipment and Technology

78. If you plan to get new or upgraded equipment or systems, remember to budget time for the learning curve or time it may take to master the new equipment and way of working. Allot time on a regular basis for a technology hardware or software upgrade day.

79. A personal computer (PC) is the #1 time-saving office equipment so get the fastest, easiest to use machine you can afford. Take the time to really master the hardware and the software that you use. Back-up your files in multiple ways, such as on a floppy disk and an Iomega® Zip disk, even storing an extra back-up disk of what is on your hard drive outside of your office.

80. Make sure you have access to a fax machine, the #2 piece of time-saving office equipment. When sending a fax to an office, get a second fax number as "back up" if the first one is always busy. If possible, have a separate phone number for the fax machine.

81. Keep up with technology and how it can revolutionalize the way you do things (and help you save time). Your competition is certainly keeping up with technology and equipment advances. Read the "Circuits" section in *The New York Times,Wall Street Journal* technology reports, or popular computing magazines.

82. Consider if a conference call will save you time and money instead of an in-person meeting involving long distance traveling.

83. When you use the Internet, focus on what you initially intended to do or find out; avoid all the tempting unrelated paths.

84. Take a typing course so you increase how fast you can type on a computer or typewriter.

85. Consider using voice recognition software: speech is recognized by special software so words are transcribed without typing.

86. If possible, have back up equipment: a second printer, computer, fax machine, or scanner. That way if any piece of equipment breaks down and needs to be repaired, you will be able to keep working without lengthy "downtime" waiting for repairs.

87. Always have at least one traditional, non-portable, phone. In that way, if you lose your electricity, you will still be able to receive or place phone calls.

88. Use devices that are convenient to carry, such as the SwissCard™ from Victorinox®, which enables you to have a scissors, pen, tweezers, and other useful tools in a handy credit-card size plastic container that will easily fit in a wallet or suitcase.

Work time

89. Whether or not your company asks for a regular progress report, create one for yourself. Look over your daily "to do" lists. Study your short- and long-term goals. Where are you achieving what you want? What needs work?

90. Take the time to stay up in your field: attend conferences, read, network, take courses or seminars, or go to school.

91. Watch for signs of burnout and stress. Adjust your work schedule, and work load, accordingly.

92. Inform callers on your voice mail of the date when you will return to your office if you will be away for one entire workday.

93. Create uninterrupted or "quiet" work time.

94. Put the time into developing and maintaining a positive relationship with those pivotal to success at work or in a business or profession: subordinates, boss, co-workers, colleagues, customers, clients, professional associations, or employees.

95. Develop and maintain a database of work-related information so you can quickly locate clients, customers, products, vendors, suppliers, as well as information, resources.

96. Remember these six business protocol principles: be on time; be discreet; be courteous, pleasant, and positive; be concerned with others, not just yourself; dress appropriately; use proper written and spoken language. [See J. Yager, *Business Protocol.*] The Internet makes any business today an international one. Find out what business protocol and time management customs, need to be considered when conducting business internationally.

97. Make sure each meeting you call is necessary. Have clear goals and a written agenda. Start, and end, on time.

98. Web sites offer the opportunity to make descriptive material such as a resume or list of available products or services available; you can save the time and cost sending out basic material.

99. From time to time, you'll do everything "right," and you will still miss a deadline. Revise your schedule since the quality of your work is more important than speed. (But if this happens more than once in a great while, work on your time management skill of scheduling so you set more realistic deadlines in the first place.)

Delegating

100. For each and every task or assignment, you need to know when, if, how, and to whom to delegate.

101. Watch for seasonal or cyclical patterns to your work flow. You might need help only at certain times of the year, or just one or two days a week.

102. Give credit to those you delegate to.

Shopping

103. Frequent stores, restaurants, service centers, or banks during non-rush or off-hour times. (You generally will not find lines at the post office when it is raining.)

104. Try to shop infrequently, stockpiling necessary supplies, and avoiding last-minute dashes for a missing item.

105. Utilize time-saving delivery services whenever possible, including shopping over the phone, by mail, or over the Internet.

106. Use a credit card as a time-saving convenience—not to get into debt—for phone, mail order, or secure Internet purchases that you might otherwise have to make in person.

107. Keep handy catalogues of your favorite mail order companies, a list of web site addresses, or phone ordering numbers.

108. Sometimes you just have to shop in person so try to make it fun: include friends, children, exercise, or eat out.

Office or household maintenance

109. Reduce clutter. Eliminate everything lacking a practical, material, or nostalgic purpose. Create a place for everything.

110. Take some time to make your home or office maintenance free. Whenever you make a purchase, consider a product's upkeep, durability, or time-saving features, such as self-cleaning ovens.

111. Intentionally invite visitors or guests to your office or home to force you to have a target cleanup date.

112. If you absolutely cannot maintain your office or home on your own, find a cleaning service to do it for you.

Holiday time

113. Create a master list of names and budget for giving gifts.

114. If your children will have holiday time off from school, try to match your work vacation time with theirs.

115. Address your holiday cards all at once or a few at a time, but finish by mid November; mail early in December.

116. If you plan to send a business holiday gift, and need to customize or imprint it with your logo, select it over the summer. You'll probably get a discount and also avoid the late Fall rush.

117. Consider sending Thanksgiving or New Year's cards as your company holiday greeting card.

118. Use the holidays as an opportunity to update your personal or business database or address book.

Personal time

119. Value your leisure time and put effort into it but without over-planning or getting obsessive about it. Make the time to do what you enjoy whether it is reading, writing, going to the movies, learning a musical instrument, traveling, or cooking.

120. Taking the time for lunch, or to prepare nutritious, satisfying dinners, or to exercise is time well spent.

121. *Really listen* to your family and get to know them.

122 . Don't let negative people drain your time or your psyche.

123. No matter how busy you are at work, try to take vacations, especially with your family when your children are young. If you cannot get away for a week or two, at least take a long weekend.

124. Relax during your personal time so you'll live longer, have more fun, and return to work refreshed.

125. Spend as much time as possible with your loved ones -- your mate, your children, your extended family, your friends.

SELECTED BIBLIOGRAPHY

ADLER, ALFRED. *What Life Should Mean To You.* NY: Putnam's, 1931, 1958.

ASLETT, DON. *Is There Life After Housework?* Cincinnati, OH: Writer's Digest Books, 1992.

BARKAS, J.L. See Yager, Jan.

BARKLEY, NELLA with E. Sandburg. *The Crystal-Barkley Guide to Taking Charge of Your Career.* NY: Workman, 1995.

BLANCHARD, KENNETH, and S. JOHNSON. *The One Minute Manager.* NY: Morrow, 1982.

BLISS, EDWIN C. *Getting Things Done.* NY: Bantam, 1976.

BOLLES, RICHARD NELSON. *What Color Is Your Parachute?* Berkeley, CA.: Ten Speed Press, 1999.

COOPER, A. M. with D. Trammell. *Time Management for Unmanageable People.* NY: Bantam, 1994.

COVEY, STEPHEN R. *7 Habits of Highly Effective People.* NY: Simon & Schuster, 1990.

_____ with A. R. MERRILL and R.. MERRILL. *First Things First.* NY: Simon & Schuster, 1994.

DAVIDSON, J. *The Complete Idiot's Guide to Managing Your Time.* NY: Alpha Books, 1996.

DAVIS, Flora. *Living Alive!* Garden City, NY: Doubleday, 1980.

DOUGLASS, M. and D. DOUGLASS. *Manage Your Time, Manage Your Work, Manage Yourself.* NY: AMACOM, 1980.

DRUCKER, PETER F. *The Practice of Management.* NY: Harper, 1954.

EISENBERG, RONNI, with KATE KELLY. *Organize Yourself!* 2nd ed. NY: Macmillan, 1997, 1986.

ELLIS, ALBERT, and W. KNAUS. *Overcoming Procrastination.* NY: NAL, 1979.

ENSIGN, PAULETTE. "110 Ideas for Organizing Your Business." San Diego, CA: OSI, 1991.

FRANCIS, J. and G. MILBOURN, JR *Human Behavior in the Work Environment.* Santa Monica, CA.: Goodyear, 1980.

FRANKL, VIKTOR E. *Man's Search for Meaning.* NY: Pocket, 1939, 1963.

FREUDENBERGER, HERBERT J., with G. RICHELSON. *Burn-Out.* Garden City, N.Y.: Doubleday, 1980.

GABARRO, JOHN J., and J. P. KOTTER. "Managing Your Boss." *HBR* (Jan-Feb 1980): 92-100.

GOLDFEIN, D. *Every Woman's Guide to Time Management.* Milbrae, CA: Les Femmes, 1977.

HALL, EDWARD T. *The Dance of Life..* Garden City, N.Y.: Anchor, 1983.

HEMPHILL, BARBARA. *Taming the Office Tiger.* Washington, D.C.: Kiplinger, 1996.

HOBBS, CHARLES R. *Time Power.* NY: Harper & Row, 1987.

JACOBS, MARCIA. *The Excuse Book.* Los Angeles, CA.: Price/Stern/Sloan, 1979.

KESSELMAN-TURKEL, J. and F. PETERSON. *Study Smarts.* Chicago, IL.: Contemporary, 1981.

KORDA, MICHAEL. *Power!* NY: Ballantine Books, 1975.

_____. *Success!* NY: Ballantine Books, 1977.

KOTTER J. P. "What Effective General Managers Really Do," *HBR* (Nov—Dec 1982):156-67.

KUBLER-ROSS, ELISABETH. *On Death and Dying.* NY: Macmillan, 1976, 1969.

KUSHNER, HAROLD S. *When Bad Things Happen to Good People..* NY: Avon, 1981.

LAKEIN, ALAN. *How to Get Control of Your Time and Your Life.* NY: NAL, 1973.

LEHMKUHL, DOROTHY. *Organizing for the Creative Person.* NY: Crown, 1994.

LEVINSON, H. "When Executives Burn Out." *Harvard Business Review* (May-June 1981): 73-81.

LOWELL, FLORENCE, and N.L. BROWNING. *Be a Guest at Your Own Party.* NY: M. Evans, 1980.

MACDERMID, S.. "Improvising New Careers." Purdue University news service, February 1999.

MACKAY, HARVEY. *Pushing the Envelope.* NY: Ballantine, 1999.

MACKENZIE, R. ALEC. *The Time Trap.* NY: McGraw-Hill, 1972.

MAYER, JEFFREY J. *Time Management for Dummies.* ® Foster City, CA: IDG Books, 1995.

MACKENZIE, R. ALEC, and KAY CRONKITE WALDO. *About Time!* NY: McGraw Hill, 1981.

MOSKOWITZ, R. *How to Organize Your Work and Your Life.* Garden City, N.Y.: Doubleday, 1981.

McQUADE, WALTER, and ANN AIKMAN. *Stress.* NY: Bantam Books, 1975.

OAKLEY, ANN. *The Sociology of Housework.* NY: Pantheon, 1974.

OFFIT, AVODAH K. *Night Thoughts.* NY: Congdon & Lattes, 1981.

ONCKEN, WILLIAM, JR., and D.. WASS. "Management Time," *HBR* (Nov-Dec 1974): 75-80.

PETERS, THOMAS and ROBERT WATERMAN JR. *In Search of Excellence.* NY: Harper, 1982.

RAND, AYN. *The Virtue of Selfishness.* NY: NAL, 1961.

RICHARDSON, G. "Learn to Structure Personal Time Needs,"*Bottom Line Personal,* 7/15/80.

RONEN, SIMCHA. *Flexible Working Hours.* NY: McGraw-Hill, 1981.

SCHIFFMAN, MURIEL. *Gestalt Self Therapy.* Berkeley, CA: Bookpeople, 1971.

_____. *Self Therapy.* Berkeley, CA: Bookpeople, 1967.

SCHUR, JULIET. The Overworked American. NY: Basic Books, 1993.

SCHUR, S. "How to Organize Your Home." 38-min. video. NY: SpaceOrganizers.

SCOTT, DRU. *How to Put More Time In Your Life.* NY: NAL, 1980.

SEDLACEK, KEITH. and M. CULLIGAN. *How to Avoid Stress Before It Kills You.* NY: Crown, 1979.

SHEERAN, JAMES J. *How to Skyrocket Your Income.* NY: Fell, 1976.

SHULEM, JULI. *Home-Based Business Mom.* Santa Barbara, CA: Newhoff Publishing, 1998.

SILBER, LEE T. *Time Management for the Creative Person.* NY: Three Rivers, 1998.

SYMONDS, MARTIN. "Victims of Violence." *AJP,* vol. 35 (Spring 1975), pp. 19-26.

TANNEN, DEBORAH. "That's Not What I Meant!" NY: Ballantine, 1987.

TAYLOR, HAROLD L. *Making Time Work For You.* NY: Dell, 1981.

TEC, LEON. *Fear of Success.* NY: NAL, 1978.

_____. *Targets.* NY: NAL, 1980.

THORPY, M. and J. YAGER. *Encyclopedia of Sleep and Sleep Disorders.* NY: Facts On File, 1991.

WAHLROOS, SVEN. *Excuses.* NY: Macmillan, 1981.

WHEELIS, ALLEN. *How People Change.* NY: Harper, 1973.

WHITE, B. and E. MADARA. *Self-Help Sourcebook.* Denville, NJ: Am. Self-Help Clearinghouse, 1998.

WILMOT, WILLIAM W. *Dyadic Communication,* 2nd edition. Reading, MA.: Addison Wesley, 1979.

WINSTON, STEPHANIE. *Getting Organized.* NY: Warner, 1978.

_____. *The Organized Executive.* Rev. ed. NY: Warner, 1994.

WINTER, ARTHUR, M.D. and RUTH WINTER. *Brain Workout.* NY: St. Martin's, 1997.

YAGER, JAN. (a/k/a J.L. Barkas*) Business Protocol,* Wiley, 1991.

_____. *Friendshifts®: The Power of Friendship and How It Shapes Our Lives.* Stamford, CT: Hannacroix Creek Books, 1997.

_____. "Is Someone Trying to Block Your Advancement at Work?"*National Business Employment Weekly,* 12/11/94. (Reprint at http://www.JanYager.com)

_____. *Making Your Office Work for You.* NY: Doubleday, 989.

_____. *Victims.* NY: Scribner's, 1978.

YOUNG, PAM, and PEGGY JONES. *Catch-up on the Kitchen.* NY: Warner, 1983.

_____. *Sidetracked Home Executives.* NY: Warner, 1981.

ZEROF, HERBERT. *Finding Intimacy.* Minneapolis, MN: Winston Press, 1978.

ZERUBAVEL, EVIATAR. *Hidden Rhythms.* Chicago, IL: University of Chicago Press, 1981.

Index

About the Author

Dr. Jan Yager is the author of more than a dozen books including these four business books: *Making Your Office Work For You* (Doubleday, 1989), the award-winning *Business Protocol* (Wiley, 1991), *How to Write Like a Professional* (Arco/Simon & Schuster, 1985), and the original *Creative Time Mangement* (Prentice Hall, Inc., 1984; Japanese edition, Mikasha Shobo, 1991), upon which this completely revised and updated second edition is based.

For more than two decades, Dr. Yager, the former J.L. Barkas, has led seminars on time management as well as conducting extensive original research in time management and workplace issues including her survey of 234 working men and women.

Dr. Yager has a Ph.D. in sociology from The City University of New York (1983), a masters in criminal justice, and a year of graduate work in psychiatric art therapy. She is a member of the National Association of Professional Organizers (NAPO), the National Speakers Association, and other associations. Dr. Yager has taught at Penn State, Temple University, and The New School.

Frequently interviewed by the media, her articles have appeared in *Parade, The New York Times, McCall's, National Business Employment Weekly, Redbook,* and *Working Woman.*

Dr. Jan Yager is a married working parent with two school-age sons who is able to achieve a successful balanced life by applying each day the creative time management principles that she developed and that are espoused in this book.

To share your comments about this book, or to find out about Dr. Yager's time management consulting or available dates for addressing your company or association, contact:

Dr. Jan Yager
P.O. Box 8038
Stamford, CT 06905-8038
(203) 968-8098 Fax (203) 968-0193
E-mail: jyager@aol.com
On the web: http://www.JanYager.com